MARK PEEL & NANCY SILVERTON AT HOME

MARK PEEL & NANCY SILVERTON AT HOME

TWO CHEFS COOK
FOR FAMILY & FRIENDS

in collaboration with Edon Waycott

WARNER BOOKS

A Time Warner Company

Grateful acknowledgment is made for permission to use the following recipes, which are reprinted, adapted, or derived from the sources below.

Homemade Yogurt, Marion Cunningham.
ANZAC Cookies, Greek Walnut Cookies, and *Kahlúa Flan*, Kerry Caloyannidis.
Crème Fraîche, Pâte Sucrée, from *Desserts*, Nancy Silverton, New York: HarperCollins, 1986.
Meyer Lemon Tart, from the *Food Lover's Guide to Paris*, Patricia Wells, New York: Workman, 1984.

Warner Books, Inc., 1271 Avenue of the Americas, New York, NY 10020

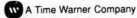 A Time Warner Company

Printed in the United States of America
First Printing: February 1994
10 9 8 7 6 5 4 3 2 1

Library of Congress Cataloging-in-Publication Data

Peel, Mark.
Mark Peel and Nancy Silverton at home : two chefs cook for family
and friends / Mark Peel and Nancy Silverton.
p.   cm.
Includes index.
ISBN 0-446-51736-4
1. Cookery.   2. Quick and easy cookery.   I. Silverton, Nancy.
II. Title.
TX714.P25   1994

641.5—dc20   92-56434
                                                         CIP

Book Design by L & G McRee

*Dedicated to Vanessa and Benjamin,
our children and our toughest critics.*

ACKNOWLEDGMENTS

We would like to thank our friends and family, who became a dedicated and professional team of tasters and commentators: Wendi Matthews, Manfred Krankl, Margy Rochlin (who always "just happened" to be in the neighborhood around dinnertime), Anne Sprecher, Brendt Rodgers, Kerry Caloyannidis; and Mark's mother, Cheryl Graf, and Nancy's parents, Doris and Larry Silverton.

Thanks are due to our agents, Maureen and Eric Lasher; to our editor, Liv Blumer, who is finally done waiting; and to Carolyn Bryant for tying up the loose ends.

Our greatest thanks must go to Edon Waycott, our collaborator, for her taste, talent, and patience.

CONTENTS

INTRODUCTION

MARK   This book was begun in 1986, after I had left Spago but before we opened Campanile. Because Nancy was still working long hours as pastry chef at Spago, I was in charge of all the meals at home. Without the pressures of a restaurant job but with all the anticipation of constructing our own restaurant, I used this opportunity to cook for Nancy, our kids, and friends and to explore some ideas for the Campanile menu.

NANCY   After Mark left Spago, our family dinners came the closest they probably ever will to the old-fashioned meals of my childhood. When I was growing up, my sister and I used to take turns setting the table every night. We'd sit around the dinner table, always in the same chairs, and share a meal with my parents, everyone discussing the day's events. I always thought that family dinners with my own children would be the same. During the year when Mark was off, we did indeed sit down together nightly as a family, and it was wonderful. Nowadays, we tend to eat the way most families do when both parents work—on the run. Our children are older, and they have their own friends and activities after school. So the memories of that year are especially precious to me.

MARK   Even with many years of experience in a professional kitchen I wasn't entirely prepared for the limitations of my kids' palates, of my own time, space, cookware, and the reality that there was no one else to do the initial preparation or clean up except me. I learned early on to clean up as I cooked to avoid facing a daunting tower of dirty dishes at the end of a meal.

NANCY   Mark did have the three heavy copper pans he purchased in France, and of course his great taste and good judgment, but I think we lacked even a simple grater and a vegetable peeler. The confines of a very small kitchen, limited equipment, and the audience of two children under six were definitely new challenges for both of us. Looking back, I'm amazed at what he was able to create.

MARK   I learned quickly that our children weren't going to wait for a complicated assembly of esoteric ingredients to become dinner. Their palates and our meager amount of time dictated that I be creative and expeditious. Children are very resistant to change. Their habits are early ingrained, such as which stuffed animal to take to bed and which lunch box is acceptable. An extensive variety of menus is not important to small children; they are often happy eating the same, familiar thing. When I was growing up, my mother had a repertoire of about eight different meals; I tried to have about fifteen so that the same main course would be served only twice a month.

NANCY   Peer pressure plays a large role in influencing what kids will eat. If her friends in kindergarten said that asparagus was awful, then Vanessa was reluctant to taste it. Mark tried to overcome this in part by involving our children in the marketing and cooking whenever possible. By explaining to them how to tell when a melon was ripe or when the pasta was done, he reinforced their interest in the meal to come.

MARK   Even when we were entertaining, some of our very best meals were the simplest ones. I remember one night we had a particularly wonderful, spontaneous meal with about six friends. The meal was assembled in stages and eaten entirely in the kitchen: thin slices of beef Carpaccio with shaved parmesan and arugula; Chicken Liver Spread mounded on top of crusty French bread; a Caesar salad that, because only the very tender inner leaves of the romaine lettuce were used, could be eaten with the fingers; a quickly seared fillet of salmon with julienned vegetables; and a simple dessert of Brandied Cherries over a good-quality purchased vanilla ice cream. It was a superb meal, which did not take hours to cook. We feel strongly that great care should always be taken in preparing a meal, but if by the time you sit down to eat you are exhausted, where is the joy?

NANCY   Another time some friends from San Francisco surprised us around dinnertime. Mark already had a chicken roasting when I got home, and I immediately thought of Chocolate Soufflé Cake for dessert, which I knew I could put together with little effort and which would taste best warm from the oven. The cake can be flavored with whiskey, but since this time the children were going to be eating with us, I used orange juice. The dark, moist cake was topped with just a dusting of powdered sugar and a dollop of whipped cream. Our guests loved the whole meal, and we loved spending time with them rather than in the kitchen. Clean-up was minimal too.

MARK   When friends stop by, I never worry as long as there is a chicken in the refrigerator. I know I have a meal. Roasted whole, surrounded by whole cloves of garlic and thickly sliced potatoes, which simmer in the juices in the pan, a chicken becomes a savory and delicious meal. I especially like to serve it with fresh spinach sautéed in a little anchovy-flavored olive oil, and some whole onions slowly caramelized in a separate pan.

NANCY   Our home life in 1986 was the primary inspiration for this book, but the food we tasted in Italy that same year was also a great influence. In late August we packed up our children and rented a little house in the Tuscany region, near Lucca. Quite often we drove around the area, stopping to eat in small villages with no landmark other than a turn in the road. One of our most memorable meals was a plain dish of fresh pasta, garnished with butter, freshly ground black pepper, and sautéed slivers of fresh porcini mushrooms. Innocent as the preparation was, the result was perfection. All of the ingredients were at their peak of quality and none was muddled by overly complex preparation. The dish so impressed us that we knew immediately that this was the kind of food we wanted to eat and cook, both at home and in our new restaurant.

MARK   When we came home, Nancy and I tried to make all of our meals similar to the ones we so enjoyed in Italy, as uncomplicated, unpretentious, and intensely flavored as possible. Even today, we find ourselves constantly striving to perfect the simple elements of each dish. Achieving this goal means straightforward cooking with our senses finely tuned. It means selecting produce at the peak of fresh-ness. It means upping our awareness of taste: allowing the pungent character of anchovies to take the edge off the acidity of a traditional tomato sauce; replacing salt with prosciutto to balance simple sweet spring peas and shallots; tripling the celery flavor in celery soup by using stalks, roots, and leaves . . .

NANCY   . . . Enhancing a custardy Caramel Rice Flan with real, moist vanilla beans instead of vanilla extract; intensifying the vivid color and taste of strawberries by cooking them in a Beaujolais wine sauce.

MARK   I feel that the flavors of a dish should be remembered, much the same way the tunes from a musical are remembered after the show is over. It is this clarity, the strength of each part and its relationship to the whole, that gives a recipe character. All this is possible in the home kitchen.

NANCY   If a recipe has only a few ingredients, then they must be the best. For the Bittersweet Chocolate Mousse, the chocolate has to be of the highest quality because the dessert is just a simple blending of eggs, honey and sugar, rum, cream, and chocolate. When I'm hungry, and Mark indulges me by cooking my favorite Peppered Steak, he uses a high-quality New York strip steak; coated with peppercorns and seared over high heat, the steak requires little adornment. Our philosophy summed up is "perfect ingredients, simple preparation."

MARK   As well as emphasizing basic ingredients, we have tried throughout this book to suggest how to use them in less familiar ways. We like everyone to recognize the ingredients in our food, but to be pleasantly surprised at how we've juxtaposed their flavors and textures. For example, Tapenade, a pungent puree of pitted Greek olives, is irresistible as an appetizer spread on a crostini of country bread, but it can also be a surprising and very delicious addition to a plate of steaming penne and fresh herbs. Tapenade gives a salty sting to salade niçoise as well. Ratatouille, another versatile basic, can be served in the expected way—warm as a vegetable for dinner—

but is equally good cold for lunch or as a bed to bake an egg on for breakfast.

NANCY In the same way, Ricotta Cheesecake is fine by itself, but when I have the extra time I like to top it with a freeform fragment of Pine Nut Brittle. The brittle, which can be eaten on its own as candy, adds another dimension to the dessert; it always surprises guests.

MARK Most people associate the meals of successful chefs with elegance, complexity, and sophistication. Thoughts of home cooking, on the other hand, usually conjure up easily prepared, very straightforward, and familiar meals. Perhaps that is why so many cookbooks written by chefs are only used on grand occasions, while for the remainder of the year they sit quietly on the shelf gathering dust. We hope we have created a usable volume written in an easily understood style that highlights interesting tastes but simple techniques. For the most part, we've used ingredients that can be purchased at neighborhood supermarkets.

NANCY Writing this book has allowed Mark and myself to give a lot of thought and consideration to exactly what cooking in the home entails. Because we have made our living as professional chefs, we needed to reconcile the techniques, methods, and ideas of restaurant cooking to the task of easily preparing a meal at home. Even though our areas of responsibility and expertise are not identical, our philosophy about food is. I trust Mark's decisions on the savory elements of the meal, and he leaves the bread and pastry creations entirely up to me. This doesn't mean that we don't openly voice opinions about the other's work; it's precisely that friction that provides the checks and balances of the restaurant menu and of our own home cooking.

MARK AND NANCY Cooking is our life and livelihood, and we are constantly striving to balance that with the love and devotion we have for our family. This means that we don't go out to eat very often, and our at-home menus are often built around such simple fare as Fettuccine with Mascarpone, Very Tomato Soup with Pasta Stars, or Japanese Flank Steak. We are two people who truly love to cook and find great satisfaction experimenting with and searching for the best possible combinations of flavors. But we are also parents of two growing children who are entering life through a restaurant's back door. Cooking at home gives us an opportunity to do what we like best for them.

—Mark Peel and Nancy Silverton

MARK PEEL & NANCY SILVERTON AT HOME

OUR PANTRY AND BASIC KITCHEN EQUIPMENT

A brief look into our pantry provides clues to what we consider important ingredients for basic home cooking.

Herbs

Best used dried are the ones with a high concentration of oil, such as bay leaves, thyme, marjoram, rosemary, and oregano. They should not be kept for more than six months. More delicate herbs, like basil, chervil, chives, parsley, and tarragon, are really best fresh. Fresh herbs are available at most supermarkets these days, but they are also very easy to grow yourself, on a sunny windowsill or in a pot just outside the kitchen door. Rosemary is so hardy that it is used as a shrub in Los Angeles city parks.

Spices

Cloves, nutmeg, cinnamon, allspice, peppercorns, and juniper berries tend to retain more flavor when left whole and ground in a spice grinder only as needed.

Vinegar

We like to keep at least four vinegars on our shelves—white wine, strong red wine, balsamic, and sherry wine. It is not necessary to buy the more expensive flavored vinegars, because you can get more taste by adding your own fresh herbs to a bottle of good-quality vinegar. Vinegars made by wineries tend to be of high quality.

Oil

A highly flavored extra-virgin olive oil is best for salad dressings and cooked pasta dishes. For sautéing, a neutral oil like safflower or canola has a clean, light taste and is far less expensive than olive oil.

Pasta

Imported brands of dried pasta are superior to domestic ones. We keep several shapes on hand—a long noodle like spaghetti or fettuccine, fusilli spirals, rotelle wagon wheels, penne quills, and tiny stars or orzo, rice-shaped pasta, to add to soups.

Chocolate

Imported couverture chocolate not only has a higher percentage of cocoa beans and cocoa butter but also is purer. Domestic chocolates are just not up to the European standards. Some of the best brands are Callebaut, Tobler, Lindt, and Suchard. Don't substitute unsweetened chocolate, which has no sugar, for bittersweet. Store chocolate well wrapped in a cool place.

Refrigerated Basics

In the refrigerator we always have a wedge of imported parmesan cheese, kalamata olives, Dijon mustard, large eggs, and unsalted butter. If all else fails, we can at least make an omelet or frittata.

We most often use whole homogenized milk in our recipes, but lowfat milk may be substituted. Don't use nonfat (skim) milk, since some milk fat may be essential to the success of a recipe. When cream is called for in a sauce, you can substitute milk, but only if the sauce does not need to be boiled. Boiled milk will curdle, but cream, because of its higher butterfat content, will not.

Cool Dry Storage

Whole heads of garlic keep a week or more if stored in a cool dry place (not the refrigerator). We also keep a supply of yellow or white onions, a few shallots, and red and russet potatoes under the same conditions. Our children, like many children, love potatoes in all guises. Nancy has even developed a sensational intense, creamy brownie that contains red potatoes (page 302).

Pots and Pans

We believe in buying the very best quality pots and pans, made of either anodized aluminum or stainless steel with aluminum bottoms, at home as well as in our restaurant. Cheaper pans are thinner, warp more easily, and do not conduct heat very well. A good sauté pan has straight sides, a high-quality metal surface, and an ovenproof handle so that the cooking may be finished in the oven. This is a way to save on burner space and to slow down the preparations if timing gets off schedule. The old black cast-iron skillet also fills a need. Well-seasoned, heavy, and indestructible, this classic is still one of our favorite pieces of cookware. Three saucepans in sizes ranging from one quart to four quarts should meet most cooks' needs. A stockpot, at least eight-quart capacity, is handy for making soups and boiling pasta. A lid is not essential since the top can always be covered with foil.

Food Processor and Standing Mixer

The most costly pieces of equipment that we recommend are a food processor and a standing mixer. Choose what you need for the type of cooking you do.

Knives

An eight- or ten-inch chef's knife, a curved or straight-bladed six-inch boning knife, and a four-inch paring knife should meet all the home cook's needs. Even the greatest knife is not much help if it isn't sharp. If you can't sharpen your knives regularly, then take them to someone who will.

Long-handled Metal Spoons

At least two of these, one of which is slotted, are convenient and practical.

Metal Tongs

It is extremely handy to have one or two pairs. Use them for turning chicken pieces without puncturing the meat, pulling baked potatoes out of the oven, flipping over sautéed slices of eggplant. Longer tongs, fourteen to sixteen inches, are perfect for the barbecue.

Wire Whisks

At least two wooden-handled wire whisks—one stiff and one flexible—are useful for whipping mashed potatoes or for whisking custard, egg whites, or cream.

Spatulas

Long-handled flexible rubber spatulas are essential for scraping out bowls and pans and for mixing ingredients together.

Zester and Grater

A metal zester with tiny holes at one end will remove the colored part of citrus peel. A four-sided grater can also remove citrus zest; it is also invaluable for grating cheese, potatoes, or zucchini.

Mandoline

One of our favorite gadgets is a small mandoline, or slicer, which makes paper-thin slices of any vegetable from potatoes to carrots. It has an adjustable blade, so you can make thicker slices of zucchini or Japanese eggplant for a ratatouille or frittata.

Metal Bowls

Large lightweight stainless steel bowls are indispensable. They are easily moved around in the kitchen, do not break, and are inexpensive. A restaurant supply store has loads of choices.

Spice Grinder

When you shop for a coffee grinder, purchase a second one to use only for spices. This is an inexpensive piece of equipment that will enhance the flavor of all your food. Whole allspice, coriander seeds, peppercorns, and cinnamon sticks freshly ground have a much more intense flavor than ground spices bought in jars.

Baking Equipment

What you need depends on the recipe, but if you like to bake you probably should have on hand, as a minimum, a muffin pan (preferably nonstick), a springform pan, a tart pan or pastry ring, a rolling pin, and several baking sheets. The best material for baking pans is aluminum.

Breakfast and Brunch

I t's curious that most people who skip breakfast during the work-week have little trouble eating breakfast on vacations, or when visiting friends, or on Sunday. So it must be not the choices available for breakfast but rather the time of day and/or the time required to prepare those choices that causes some people to forgo the day's most important meal. Although we pour out as many bowls of Cheerios for our kids as any parents, we also like to encourage variety. Muffins, potatoes, melted cheese on whole-grain toast, fruits, and granola with yogurt are satisfying, healthy, and simple. Even on school-day mornings, we can quickly put together Banana Poppyseed Muffins and scramble eggs before carpool.

Ideally, the first foods you eat in the morning should be light but also able to give you that all-important boost of energy. For instance, fresh fruit (a quick natural sugar source) combined with grains (complex carbohydrates) is a good balanced breakfast that will sustain you for hours. Potatoes, too, are a great breakfast food; they are loaded with vitamins, carbohydrates, and fiber (if unpeeled) and are very comforting to someone who has trouble looking squarely at an egg at 7 A.M. Our family enjoys Potato Pancakes with Caramelized Apples on Saturday mornings, when everyone eats in pajamas and the newspaper is spread across the breakfast table.

Weekend mornings allow for menus with longer preparation time and perhaps more family unity. The aroma of Nancy's Breakfast Tarte Tatin baking in the oven would awaken even the most confirmed sleepy-head. And Oven-puffed French Toast is always a hit with our children and their friends on weekends when there are sleepovers; it's especially easy to make because the batter is prepared the night before.

Weekends are also the time for inviting grown-up friends over for brunch. This is a favorite way of entertaining for many people, and for good reason. Omelets, frittatas, and other egg dishes are generally quite easy to make; they are perfect brunch fare when accompanied by freshly squeezed juices, espresso or cappuccino, and a basket of warm breakfast breads or muffins.

Poached Eggs with Chicory and Bacon

Our children both love salads, which, admittedly, don't sound like breakfast fare. Mark devised this dish to please them, but the tastes and textures are definitely sophisticated enough for adults. This recipe is his adaptation of a salad served at Michael's Restaurant in Santa Monica, California.

**2 large heads of chicory or curly endive
6 ounces slab bacon or 6 thick-sliced bacon strips
6 tablespoons lemon juice
½ teaspoon coarse salt
2 tablespoons Dijon mustard
¼ cup vegetable oil
¼ teaspoon coarsely ground black pepper
8 eggs**

1. Pull off and discard the outer, dark green, tough leaves of the chicory. Separate the tender pale yellow leaves from the core, wash well, and chop into 2-inch pieces. Dry with paper towels and set aside.

2. If the skin is still on the bacon, cut it off, then cut the bacon into ¼-inch strips. Cut the strips into ¼-inch pieces. Because of the thickness of the slab, you should then have pieces ¼ × ¼ × 1 inch. If the bacon is presliced, simply cut into ¼-inch pieces.

3. In a medium skillet sauté the bacon pieces over moderate heat until lightly browned. Remove to paper towels to drain. Pour the rendered bacon fat into a glass measuring cup. Return 3 tablespoons of the fat to the skillet.

4. Fill another, larger skillet with water to within 1 inch of the top. Add 2 tablespoons of the lemon juice and place over moderate heat. Meanwhile, warm the bacon fat over low heat and whisk in the remaining 4 tablespoons of lemon juice, and the salt, mustard, oil, and pepper. Turn off the heat but continue whisking until the dressing is emulsified.

5. When the water is at a simmer, carefully crack the eggs into the pan and poach for 3 to 4 minutes. With a slotted spoon remove the eggs to a plate, and trim any ragged edges around the whites.

6. Cover 4 plates evenly with the chicory and center 2 poached eggs on each. Scatter the bacon over the eggs and spoon some of the dressing over all. Serve immediately.

Serves 4

Soft-boiled Eggs with Stilton Butter Sauce

For some reason we tend to associate very proper breakfasts with the English. Stilton cheese is one of England's trademarks, and here it gives balance and sharpness to perfectly cooked soft-boiled eggs, perhaps served in beautiful china egg cups. The sauce may also be spooned over poached eggs on English muffins.

This comforting egg dish is also one of our favorite late-night suppers after the children are asleep. Toasted slices of pain de mie *or baguette and a green salad are all we need to complete the repast.*

STILTON BUTTER SAUCE

2 tablespoons water
1 teaspoon white wine or cider vinegar
4 tablespoons (½ stick) unsalted butter, cut into 4 pieces
1 ounce Stilton cheese, or to taste
¼ teaspoon coarsely ground black pepper

4 soft-boiled eggs, cooked to taste

GARNISH
Finely chopped fresh chives

1. To make the sauce, bring the water and vinegar to a full boil in a small skillet. Whisk in the butter until melted. Turn off the heat and crumble the cheese into the mixture. Whisk until smooth and add pepper.
2. Snip off the tops of the eggshells with an egg cutter or sharp knife and gently spoon in the sauce. Or break 2 eggs each into 2 bowls and top with sauce. Sprinkle with chives.

Serves 2

Baked Eggs on Ratatouille

This is a colorful, very satisfying brunch dish, especially when accompanied by thick slices of toast. Ratatouille is a traditional French dish consisting of five vegetables of various colors and textures. To ensure that the vegetables are cooked perfectly, we sauté each one individually. In this recipe, using two skillets at once cuts the cooking time in half. The ratatouille can be cooked and assembled up to two days before baking with the eggs; it only gets better. Leftover ratatouille can be served cold for lunch with crusty French bread.

2 medium Japanese eggplants, unpeeled and cut into ¼-inch
slices
⅔ cup olive oil
6 Italian plum tomatoes, seeded and coarsely chopped (canned
tomatoes, well drained, can be substituted in winter)
3 medium zucchini, ends removed, cut in half lengthwise, then
cut into ½-inch pieces
Coarse salt
Coarsely ground black pepper
1 medium red bell pepper, stemmed, seeded, and cut into
julienne strips
1 medium onion, chopped
4 large garlic cloves, minced
2 tablespoons finely chopped fresh basil
1 tablespoon finely chopped fresh thyme or 1 teaspoon dried
thyme
8 eggs

1. Preheat the oven to 250° F.

2. Place the eggplant slices on an ungreased baking sheet and dry in the oven for 20 minutes. Remove the eggplant and raise the temperature to 350° F.

3. In each of 2 medium skillets heat 1½ tablespoons olive oil; add the tomatoes to one and zucchini to the other. Sprinkle the vegetables with salt and pepper. Sauté over high heat for 2 minutes. Transfer the tomatoes to a serving bowl. Continue cooking the zucchini for 2 minutes more, until lightly browned but still firm. Add to the tomatoes.

4. Pour another 1½ tablespoons of the olive oil into each skillet and place the peppers in one, the onions in the other. Sprinkle with salt and pepper. Sauté until barely tender and lightly browned. Add to the vegetables in the serving bowl. Do not stir.

5. Pour another 1½ tablespoons olive oil into one skillet and lightly brown the eggplant slices. Place the eggplant slices on top of the other vegetables. Add the garlic, basil, thyme, and remaining olive oil. Fold together very gently. Set aside at room temperature, or refrigerate if not using the same day.

6. Fill a roasting pan, large enough to hold four 4- to 6-ounce ramekins, with 1 inch of hot water. Into each ramekin spoon enough ratatouille to come within 1 inch of the top. With the back of a spoon, make an indentation, and break 2 eggs into it. Sprinkle with salt and pepper. Place the ramekins in the water bath and cover loosely with a tent of foil.

7. Place in the oven and bake until the eggs are soft-set, about 20 minutes. The eggs will continue to firm up after being removed from the oven. Serve immediately.

Serves 4

Creamy Scrambled Eggs with Porcini Mushrooms

One of our pet peeves is overcooked, rubbery scrambled eggs. Since eggs continue to set after they are removed from the heat, assemble everyone at the table before pouring the whisked eggs into the pan. This version incorporates the woodsy flavor of porcini mushrooms. For a special Sunday breakfast serve these eggs with a chunk of smoked whitefish.

8 eggs
1 garlic clove, minced
½ teaspoon chopped fresh thyme or ¼ teaspoon dried thyme
¼ teaspoon coarse salt
½ leek, white part only, split and well washed
3 tablespoons olive oil
¼ ounce dried porcini mushrooms, soaked in hot water to
      cover for 30 minutes
1½ pounds fresh spinach, washed and stemmed
3 tablespoons unsalted butter

   1. Crack the eggs into a medium bowl and add the garlic, thyme, and salt. Whisk lightly with a fork and set aside.
   2. Cut the leek into ¼-inch half-circles and sauté over medium heat in 1 tablespoon of the olive oil. Transfer to the bowl with the eggs.
   3. Drain the mushrooms, squeeze dry, and sauté in 1 tablespoon of the olive oil just until the edges begin to curl. Add to the egg mixture.

4. Heat the remaining tablespoon of olive oil and sauté the spinach just until it wilts. Remove to a platter and keep warm.

5. Melt the butter in the same pan, and when it sizzles, pour in the egg mixture. Stir constantly over medium heat.

6. When about half of the eggs are "clumped," less than a minute, spoon onto the bed of spinach. The eggs will continue to set. They will still be creamy by the time they are eaten.

Serves 4

Omelet with Eggplant-and-Tomato Chutney

The filling for this omelet is thick and red and will appeal to the secret society of people who like ketchup with eggs. Leftover eggplant-tomato mixture will also go well with grilled fish. Leftover chutney can be stored, covered, in the refrigerator for up to a week.

CHUTNEY

¼ cup olive oil
1 medium onion, finely chopped
1½ cups finely chopped unpeeled eggplant
3 large garlic cloves, minced
8 large white mushrooms, stems removed, finely chopped
1 teaspoon coarse salt
½ teaspoon coarsely ground black pepper
¼ teaspoon crushed red pepper
1 28-ounce can chopped tomatoes or whole tomatoes finely
    chopped, drained and liquid reserved
1 teaspoon dried oregano
1 teaspoon dried thyme
3 tablespoons sherry wine vinegar or red wine vinegar

OMELET

6 large eggs
¼ teaspoon coarse salt
¼ teaspoon coarsely ground black pepper
2 tablespoons unsalted butter

1. In a large skillet over moderate heat sauté the onion, eggplant, and garlic in the olive oil until the eggplant is very soft. Add the mushrooms, salt, pepper, and crushed red pepper and stir to combine. Simmer until all the juices have evaporated. Add the tomatoes, 3 tablespoons of the reserved tomato liquid, and the oregano, thyme, and vinegar. Cook, uncovered, until most of liquid has evaporated. Lower the heat as far as possible, cover, and cook for 20 to 30 minutes. Set aside to cool slightly before using in the omelet.

2. Whisk the eggs, salt, and pepper in a medium bowl. In a nonstick

skillet or omelet pan heat 1 tablespoon of the butter. When it sizzles, pour in half of the egg mixture. As the bottom and sides begin to set, pull the eggs toward the center of the pan with a spatula. When the eggs are no longer liquid but still soft, spread 2 tablespoons of the eggplant-tomato mixture down the center.

3. Gently loosen the sides of the omelet with a spatula, if necessary, and slide onto a plate, folding the eggs in half over the filling. Repeat with the remaining eggs to make a second omelet.

Serves 2

Zucchini Frittata with Blue Cheese

The frittata is a popular egg-and-vegetable dish in Spain, Italy, and southern France. We are fond of it because it's a great way to use seasonal fresh vegetables, as well as whatever we happen to have in our refrigerator. Yellow summer squash, thick strips of red bell pepper, thinly sliced Japanese eggplant, mushrooms, or leeks can be substituted for the zucchini.

4 eggs
1 teaspoon chopped fresh thyme or ½ teaspoon dried thyme
¼ teaspoon coarse salt
½ teaspoon coarsely ground black pepper
2 garlic cloves, minced
3 tablespoons olive oil
2 medium zucchini, cut into ⅛-inch rounds
2 to 3 ounces blue cheese or gorgonzola, crumbled

1. In a medium bowl whisk together the eggs, thyme, salt, pepper, and garlic.

2. Pour the olive oil into an 8- or 9-inch cast-iron or other ovenproof skillet and arrange the zucchini slices in concentric circles covering the bottom of the pan, overlapping each slice about halfway. Place the pan over high heat and cook until the zucchini begins to brown around the edges.

3. Carefully pour the egg mixture on top and cook until the outer 1 inch of eggs is set. Sprinkle with crumbled cheese and place under the broiler approximately 4 inches from the heat. Watch carefully to avoid burning. The frittata is done when it is puffed and golden brown, about 3 minutes. The center will be somewhat creamy because of the melted cheese.

Serves 4

Potato, Fennel, and Garlic Frittata

This is a good weekend dish, either for Sunday brunch or for supper. Although the flavor is better if the eggs and seasonings are allowed to sit overnight, a few hours will suffice.

1 medium fennel bulb
6 eggs
1 teaspoon chopped fresh tarragon or ½ teaspoon dried
   tarragon
1 garlic clove, minced
¼ teaspoon coarsely ground black pepper
3 tablespoons olive oil
1 medium red potato, peeled and cut into 1-inch cubes
6 large garlic cloves, sliced into thirds
¾ teaspoon coarse salt
1 tablespoon unsalted butter
3 to 4 ounces Jarlsberg or Swiss cheese, cut into ½ ✕ 3-inch
   strips

1. Remove the top feathery greens from the fennel bulb, chopping enough to equal 1 tablespoon and reserving the remainder whole.

2. In a medium bowl whisk together the eggs, chopped fennel greens, tarragon, minced garlic, and pepper. Set aside, covered, for 1 hour or refrigerate overnight.

3. Remove any tough outer stalks from the fennel and cut the bulb horizontally into ¼-inch slices. In a 9- or 10-inch ovenproof skillet heat 2 tablespoons of the olive oil and sauté the potatoes and fennel over moderate heat until tender, about 10 minutes. Remove to a plate. Add the sliced garlic and sauté briefly. Return the vegetables to the skillet with the garlic, sprinkle with salt, and toss together for 1 minute. Transfer all the vegetables to a plate and wipe the skillet clean with a paper towel.

4. Melt the butter with the remaining 1 tablespoon of olive oil and pour in the egg mixture. Do not stir the eggs. Cook over low heat for 1 to 2 minutes, or until the edges begin to set, then spread the vegetables

over the top. Arrange the cheese strips like spokes of a wheel over the vegetables, place under the broiler, and broil just until the cheese melts.

5. Carefully slide the frittata onto a serving plate, cheese side up. Garnish with reserved fennel greens.

Serves 4

Twelve-Egg Frittata with Bacon and Bitter Greens

Bacon and greens—two Southern favorites—are combined here in an intensely flavored frittata. This is one egg dish that is just as good warm, at room temperature, or chilled. Take slices on your next picnic, accompanied perhaps by Roasted Potato Salad (page 104).

12 slices bacon, cut into ½-inch pieces
1 large bunch mustard greens (about ½ pound)
12 eggs
¾ cup milk or half-and-half
¼ teaspoon coarsely ground black pepper
1½ tablespoons capers, chopped
4 ounces blue cheese
2 tablespoons unsalted butter

1. In a 14-inch ovenproof skillet fry the bacon over moderate heat until browned but not crisp. Remove with a slotted spoon to paper towels to drain. Discard all but 1 tablespoon of the fat in the pan.

2. Wash the mustard greens and remove and discard the stems. Cut the leaves into 1-inch strips. Sauté in the reserved bacon fat just until wilted. Remove from the pan, squeeze out any liquid that might make the eggs runny, and set aside.

3. In a large bowl whisk together the eggs, milk, pepper, capers, and half of the cheese. Stir in the bacon and mustard greens.

4. Melt the butter in the skillet over high heat and pour in the egg mixture. Crumble the remaining cheese on top. Cook until the edges are set. Place in the broiler 4 inches from the heat and broil until lightly browned but still soft in the center. Remove from the oven and allow to stand for 5 minutes before serving.

5. Carefully slide the frittata onto a serving platter or serve directly from the skillet.

Serves 6

Gruyère and Onion Tart with Potato Crust

Many home cooks shy away from making pastry for a quiche, but this breakfast/brunch/lunch tart has grated potatoes pressed into an ovenproof skillet for a crust. Waxy white or red potatoes are a better choice than russet because they do not become mealy when cooked. This recipe contains three of our kids' favorite foods—bacon, potatoes, and eggs.

5 waxy white or red potatoes (about 2½ pounds)
½ pound pancetta or slab bacon
2 medium white onions, finely chopped
Coarse salt
Sugar
3 garlic cloves, minced
½ tablespoon chopped fresh rosemary or 2 teaspoons crumbled
    dried rosemary
Coarsely ground black pepper
2 tablespoons vegetable oil
3 cups grated gruyère cheese (about ¾ pound)
5 eggs
2 cups heavy cream or half-and-half
Freshly grated nutmeg

1. Boil the potatoes in water to cover for 5 minutes. Drain and cool for 10 minutes, then peel. Set aside to cool.

2. Cut the pancetta or bacon into ½-inch dice and slowly brown in a 10- to 12-inch ovenproof skillet until almost all the fat has been rendered. Transfer to paper towels to drain.

3. In the remaining fat in the skillet cook the onions with a pinch of salt and sugar over medium heat until soft and lightly browned. Stir in the garlic and rosemary. Remove from the pan.

4. Preheat the oven to 350° F.

5. Grate the potatoes using the large holes of a grater or in a food processor fitted with a shredding disk. Season with a little salt and pepper. Grease the skillet with the vegetable oil and press the potatoes against the bottom and sides of it. Place over high heat and cook just until the bottom of the potatoes begins to brown, about 5 minutes. Spread the onion mixture over the potatoes. Sprinkle with the pancetta and gruyère.

6. In a bowl beat the eggs with the cream until blended. Season with salt, pepper, and nutmeg. Pour over the onions and bake for 30 to 35 minutes, or until puffed and browned.

7. Allow to stand for 10 minutes before cutting into wedges.

Serves 6

Goat Cheese Soufflé

Don't be put off by the word "soufflé"——this is very easy to make and not at all fragile, more like a pudding really. Accompanied by fresh fruit and homemade sausage patties, it makes a delicious brunch. But don't exclude the idea of serving it as a first course followed by grilled fish or seafood.

1½ cups milk
3 garlic cloves
3 marjoram sprigs
6 tablespoons (¾ stick) unsalted butter
6 tablespoons flour
¾ pound goat cheese, such as montrachet
4 eggs, separated
Coarse salt
1 teaspoon chopped fresh marjoram
½ teaspoon coarsely ground black pepper

1. In a small saucepan heat the milk with the garlic and marjoram sprigs just to a boil, turn off the heat, and allow to steep for 10 minutes. Remove and discard the garlic and marjoram.

2. In a medium saucepan over medium heat melt the butter and whisk in the flour. Slowly whisk in the warm milk and stir until very smooth. Add two-thirds of the cheese and whisk until incorporated. Set aside to cool to room temperature. (The soufflé base may be prepared ahead to this point several hours before serving and refrigerated.) Stir in the egg yolks.

3. Preheat the oven to 375° F. Liberally butter a 2-quart straight-sided shallow baking or gratin dish.

4. Beat the egg whites with a pinch of salt until they hold soft peaks. Do not beat until dry. Thoroughly fold a quarter of the whites into the cheese mixture. Sprinkle in the chopped marjoram and pepper, stir to combine, and fold in the remaining whites. Pour into the dish. Dot with the remaining cheese.

5. Place in the center of the oven. Bake for 30 minutes, or until the top is puffed and golden brown. Serve immediately.

Serves 6

Potato Pancakes with Caramelized Apples

This is one of our family's very favorite weekend breakfast dishes. Lightly sweetened apple slices are coupled with crisp, lacy pancakes. For a complete breakfast, you can accompany the pancakes with sausage patties or links and a bran muffin. Or serve them with soft-boiled eggs, which take only minutes to prepare.

If you're peeling and shredding the potatoes in advance, place them in a bowl of ice water so they don't discolor. If you're peeling and slicing the apples in advance, place them in a bowl of lemon water so they don't discolor.

2 egg whites
Coarse salt
½ teaspoon coarsely ground white pepper
3 tablespoons flour
3 tablespoons cornstarch
3 medium red or white potatoes (about 1½ pounds)
¾ cup very thinly sliced onion (½ pound)
4 tablespoon (½ stick) unsalted butter
2 tart apples, such as pippin or Granny Smith, peeled, cored,
    and cut into ¼-inch slices
2 tablespoons sugar
¾ cup vegetable oil
½ cup sour cream

1. Beat the egg whites with ¼ teaspoon salt until stiff peaks form. Slowly beat in the pepper, flour, and cornstarch until the mixture resembles a thick paste.

2. Peel and shred the potatoes in a food processor fitted with a medium shredding blade. Or cut the potatoes into ¼-inch slices, then into matchstick-size pieces. Add the potatoes and two-thirds of the sliced onions to the egg mixture and stir to coat well. Set aside.

3. In a medium skillet melt the butter over medium-high heat and add the remaining onion. Cook until soft. Add the apples, sugar, and a pinch of salt and cook, stirring often, until the apples are lightly browned. Keep warm over very low heat while making the pancakes.

4. Pour 2 tablespoons of the oil into an 8-inch skillet and heat until very hot. Measure out about ¾ cup of the potato mixture and pour it into the pan, spreading quickly to the edges with a spatula. There should be holes in the pancake; do not make it solid. Sauté for 3 to 5 minutes. Check the bottom to see if it is well browned, then loosen any stuck

edges and flip it over. Cook 3 to 5 minutes more, until crisp. Serve immediately or keep in a warm oven until all the pancakes are completed. For each pancake heat 2 tablespoons of oil in the skillet before adding more potato mixture.

5. To serve, place a pancake on a plate, spoon 1½ to 2 tablespoons sour cream on the center, and top with a heaping tablespoon of warm apples.

Serves 4

Variation: To make 1 large pancake, cook all of the potato mixture in ⅓ cup of hot oil in a 12-inch skillet until very browned on the bottom. Turn carefully and cook the second side. Transfer to a large round platter, spread with ½ cup of sour cream in a 4-inch circle, and top with all the apples. Cut into wedges to serve.

Breakfast Rice Pancakes

When we're serving rice for a family dinner, we often make an extra two cups to be able to make these tasty pancakes in the morning. Equally good with white or brown rice, they'll remind you of cinnamon-scented rice pudding. Serve them with butter and warm maple syrup.

1 cup all-purpose flour
1½ teaspoons baking powder
1 teaspoon coarse salt
1 teaspoon ground cinnamon
1 teaspoon grated orange zest
½ teaspoon grated lemon zest
¼ cup sugar
1½ cups (packed) cooked rice
2 egg yolks
2 tablespoons unsalted butter, melted
2 egg whites, stiffly beaten

1. In a medium mixing bowl combine the flour, baking powder, salt, cinnamon, orange and lemon zest, sugar, and rice. Stir in the egg yolks, butter, and beaten egg whites.

2. Lightly grease a griddle or frying pan and place over medium heat until hot. Drop in the batter, ¼ cup at a time. Cook until bubbles appear on the top, then turn over. Serve immediately.

Serves 4 to 6

Light Lemon Pancakes

Just about the time of the Jewish holiday Hanukkah, our friend Judy Zeidler called and asked if we would create a latke *(pancake) recipe for an article she was writing for the* Los Angeles Times. *We remembered a dessert pancake Nancy had made at Spago and tried to duplicate the lightness and delicate texture. After trying (and eating) many variations, which included raspberries, blueberries, and sautéed apples, we decided our favorite was this one, created by Mark.*

½ cup all-purpose flour
1 teaspoon grated lemon zest
5 tablespoons sugar
½ teaspoon coarse salt
4 eggs, separated
⅓ cup milk
2 tablespoons unsalted butter, melted
1 teaspoon pure vanilla extract
Juice of 1 lemon
Confectioners' sugar
Orange marmalade for serving

1. In a medium bowl stir together the flour, lemon zest, sugar, and salt. Make a well in the center and pour in the egg yolks, milk, butter, and vanilla. Using a fork, gradually incorporate the liquids into the dry mixture.

2. In a separate mixing bowl beat the egg whites until stiff but not dry. Gently fold into the batter until well combined.

3. Lightly butter a skillet or griddle and pour in approximately ¼ cup of batter for each pancake. Turn when small bubbles appear.

4. Squeeze a little fresh lemon juice over each pancake, dust with confectioners' sugar, and serve with a spoonful of the best orange marmalade you can find.

Serves 4

Oven-puffed French Toast

On the weekends, when our children invite their friends to sleep over, we like to serve this French toast as a special treat. Everything can be assembled the night before, making breakfast time pleasantly leisurely. Don't be afraid of the beer in the batter; the alcohol evaporates, leaving the French toast with a marvelous flavor and a lacy texture.

One 1-pound day-old baguette, unsliced
10 eggs
½ cup all-purpose flour
6 tablespoons sugar
½ teaspoon baking powder
2 teaspoons pure vanilla extract
1 cup milk
1 cup beer, preferably dark
Coarse salt
8 tablespoons (1 stick) unsalted butter
Butter for serving
Maple syrup for serving

1. Cut the bread into ¾-inch-thick slices and place in one or more dishes large enough to hold the slices in a single layer. In a bowl whisk together the eggs, flour, sugar, baking powder, vanilla, milk, beer, and a pinch of salt. Pour over the bread slices, turning to soak both sides. Cover with plastic wrap and refrigerate overnight or for at least 1 hour.

2. Preheat the oven to 350° F.

3. In a very large ovenproof skillet melt the butter over medium heat. Add the soaked bread and brown on one side. Turn the bread over and place the skillet in the oven for 10 to 12 minutes, until the toast is puffed and golden brown on the bottom. Do in batches if necessary.

4. Serve immediately with additional butter and maple syrup.

Serves 4

Granola

Granola, once the health breakfast of Flower Children, has become adulterated commercially with too much sugar, corn syrup, and saturated oils. It takes little effort and time to make a far more flavorful and nutritious version at home. Make the whole amount, even though it seems like a large quantity, since it freezes well. You can substitute two cups of mixed dried fruits of your choice for the ones specified in the recipe. Our children love this, especially stirred into Homemade Yogurt (recipe follows).

4 cups old-fashioned rolled oats (not quick-cooking)
¾ cup raw pumpkin seeds
¾ cup unsalted raw sunflower seeds
1 cup coarsely chopped unblanched almonds
½ cup wheat germ
½ cup powdered nonfat dry milk
1 tablespoon ground cinnamon
2 teaspoons ground nutmeg
¼ teaspoon ground cloves
2 teaspoons pure vanilla extract
¾ cup safflower oil
½ cup maple syrup
½ cup honey or malt syrup (available in health food stores)
½ cup dried apricots, finely chopped
½ cup dried figs, finely chopped
½ cup golden raisins
½ cup black raisins

1. Preheat the oven to 350° F.

2. Stir together the oats, seeds, almonds, wheat germ, dry milk, cinnamon, nutmeg, cloves, and vanilla. Set aside.

3. In a small saucepan over medium heat stir together the oil, maple syrup, and honey. Pour over the oat mixture and toss with your hands or a wooden spoon until all the ingredients are moistened. Spread on a cookie sheet and bake for 30 minutes, stirring once. The edges tend to brown first, so stir carefully. When lightly browned, remove from the oven and cool to room temperature. Loosen from the pan in chunks and add the dried fruits. Seal in freezer lock bags or airtight tins.

Makes about 9 cups

Homemade Yogurt

Mounded on top of granola with fresh fruit, yogurt is a nutritious beginning for the day. Very simple to prepare and far less expensive than storebought, homemade yogurt can also substitute for sour cream on top of a baked potato. How tangy it is depends on how long it is left to stand at room temperature. Start with lowfat or whole milk and the freshest Bulgarian-style yogurt you can find as a starter. This is Marion Cunningham's recipe, and we thank her for sharing it with us.

1 quart lowfat or whole milk
2 tablespoons Bulgarian-style plain yogurt

Heat the milk to the boiling point for just 1 minute. Cool to 115° F. (a thermometer is essential here). Gently stir in the yogurt (the starter) and pour the mixture into a glass or ceramic bowl. Cover tightly with plastic wrap and set in a warm spot. An oven with just the pilot light on or its electric light burning is ideal. Or put it in a warm corner of the kitchen with a towel draped over to protect it from drafts. The yogurt should be ready in 5 to 8 hours. Tilt the bowl to see if it holds together. It should then be chilled 3 hours to firm up even more. If the yogurt sets too long a time or if you used too much starter, it will be watery. It will keep refrigerated for about a week.

Makes 1 quart

Buttermilk–Orange Biscuits

You may be averse to getting out the bottle of rum in the morning, but the small amount called for here has a magical effect. Together with orange juice, it plumps the raisins and gives them an intriguing flavor. Your kids will never know. They'll just think these biscuits are delicious.

⅓ cup orange juice
⅓ cup rum
1 teaspoon pure vanilla extract
½ cup raisins
2 cups all-purpose flour
1 tablespoon sugar
2 teaspoons baking powder
1 teaspoon baking soda
1 teaspoon coarse salt
8 tablespoons (1 stick) cold unsalted butter, cut into 8 pieces
⅓ cup buttermilk
1 teaspoon grated orange zest
Milk
5 teaspoons sugar

1. In a small bowl stir together the orange juice, rum, vanilla, and raisins. Set aside for 10 to 15 minutes while preparing the biscuits.

2. Preheat the oven to 375° F.

3. In a food processor fitted with the metal blade combine the flour, sugar, baking powder, baking soda, and salt. Pulse to combine. Add the butter and process until the mixture looks like coarse meal.

4. Drain the liquid from the raisins into a measuring cup and reserve ⅓ cup. Add with the buttermilk to the flour mixture in the processor. Add the raisins and orange zest. Pulse just to dampen the dry ingredients. The dough will be sticky.

5. Remove the dough from the bowl and knead 10 times on a well-floured surface. Pat into an 8-inch round, ½ inch thick. Cut 8 biscuits with a floured 2½-inch cutter. Fold the scraps together and cut 2 more biscuits. Place on a lightly greased baking sheet, 1 inch apart. Brush the tops with milk and sprinkle each with ½ teaspoon sugar.

6. Bake for 15 to 18 minutes, until the tops are lightly browned.

Makes 10 biscuits

Breakfast Tarte Tatin

A variation on the classic French dessert, our homestyle caramelized apple treat uses a simple buttermilk biscuit dough. Preparation time is not long; this upside-down creation can even be made the night before.

¾ **cup sugar**
¼ **cup water**
5 **or 6 Red or Golden Delicious apples**
2 **tablespoons lemon juice stirred with cold water**
1½ **cups all-purpose flour**
2 **teaspoons baking powder**
½ **teaspoon baking soda**
¼ **teaspoon coarse salt**
6 **tablespoons cold unsalted butter, cut into 8 pieces**
½ **cup buttermilk**

1. Preheat the oven to 400° F.

2. In an 8- or 9-inch cast-iron or other heavy ovenproof skillet mix together the sugar and water. Place over low heat and, without stirring, melt the sugar until it becomes mahogany-colored. This will take 5 to 7 minutes.

3. Meanwhile, peel, core, and quarter the apples. Drop into the lemon water.

4. When the caramel is ready, raise the heat to medium and place the apples, cut side down with the stem end pointing toward the center, around the edge of the pan, wedging them in as tightly as possible. To fill the center space, cut pieces in half crosswise and place side by side. Apples will shrink a great deal while cooking so it's important to fit in as many as possible. The juices from the apples will dissolve any caramel that has hardened. Cook the apples for 10 minutes.

5. While the apples are cooking, make the batter by placing the flour, baking powder, baking soda, and salt in a food processor fitted with the metal blade. Pulse to combine. Add the butter and process until the mixture resembles coarse meal. Add the buttermilk and process just until the dry ingredients are moistened. The mixture will resemble a stiff biscuit dough.

6. Remove the apples from the heat and drop the batter on top by large spoonfuls, smoothing with the back of the spoon to distribute as evenly as possible. Place on a baking sheet in the oven.

7. Bake for 15 to 18 minutes, or until the biscuit is golden brown and slightly risen. Remove from the oven and allow to rest for 1 minute. Cover with a serving plate and invert the skillet, allowing the juices to drip onto the apples for 1 minute.

Serves 6

Crème Fraîche Coffeecake

This wonderfully rich coffeecake has been reinvented almost as many times as there are cookbooks. The crumb is moist, dense, and full of butter flavor, and the layer of streusel is everyone's favorite combination of pecans, brown sugar, and cinnamon. Close your eyes, and you can probably recall eating something very similar in your childhood. Whenever Nancy makes this at home, the tantalizing aroma fills the apartment, and before the coffeecake has even cooled we're breaking off big hunks with our hands.

½ pound (2 sticks) unsalted butter, at room temperature
2 cups granulated sugar
2 eggs, beaten
2 cups Crème Fraîche (page 248)
1 tablespoon pure vanilla extract
1 tablespoon finely chopped lemon zest
2 cups all-purpose flour
1 tablespoon baking powder
¼ teaspoon coarse salt
¾ cup light brown sugar
2 cups coarsely chopped pecans, lightly toasted for 10 minutes
     in a 350° F. oven
4 teaspoons ground cinnamon

1. Preheat the oven to 350° F. Butter a 10-inch Bundt pan.
2. In the large bowl of an electric mixer cream together the butter and sugar until light and fluffy. Add the eggs and beat until well blended. On low speed add the Crème Fraîche, vanilla, and lemon zest.

3. In a small bowl stir together by hand the flour, baking powder, and salt. Add to the butter mixture, beating just until blended. In another small bowl stir together by hand the brown sugar, pecans, and cinnamon for the streusel.

4. Pour half the batter into the Bundt pan. Sprinkle with half the streusel. Pour in the remaining batter, spreading with the back of a spoon to cover the streusel as much as possible. Top with the remaining streusel.

5. Bake for about 1 hour, or until a toothpick inserted into the center comes out clean. Remove from the oven and invert onto a serving plate. Serve warm.

Serves 10

Café Bran Muffins

These moist and flavorful muffins require nothing other than, perhaps, butter or honey. We serve them at our café and are sure to get complaints from our loyal customers whenever they are not available. For some people, breakfast just isn't the same without coffee and a bran muffin. Toasting the bran first gives it a nuttier flavor and richer color.

1½ cups black raisins
1½ cups water
2 cups unprocessed bran
½ cup buttermilk
½ cup vegetable oil
1 whole egg
1 egg white
½ cup all-purpose flour
4 tablespoons whole wheat flour
½ cup (packed) light brown sugar
1 teaspoon grated orange zest
1 teaspoon baking powder
1 teaspoon baking soda
¼ teaspoon coarse salt

1. Preheat the oven to 375° F. Grease 10 standard-size muffin cups or line with paper liners.

2. In a small saucepan stir together 1 cup of the raisins and 1 cup of water and simmer on low heat until all the water is absorbed, about 15 minutes. Place in a food processor fitted with the metal blade and process until pureed.

3. Spread the bran on a cookie sheet and toast for 8 to 10 minutes, until well browned, stirring once. Leave the oven turned on at the same setting. Pour the bran into a large bowl, and add the buttermilk and remaining ½ cup of water. Stir to moisten. Add the raisin puree and stir well.

4. With a wooden spoon or whisk beat in the oil, egg, and egg white. Add the flours, brown sugar, orange zest, baking powder, baking soda, salt, and remaining ½ cup of raisins. Stir together until all the ingredients

are well combined. The batter will be light and moist. Fill the muffin cups, mounding the batter slightly.

5. Bake for 20 to 22 minutes, until the muffins are cracked and browned on top. Remove the pan from the oven and allow the muffins to cool in the pan for 5 minutes.

Makes 10 muffins

Applesauce Muffins with Dried Fruit

Applesauce adds moisture and browned butter adds a nutty flavor to these naturally sweetened muffins. Any mixture of soft dried fruit will do.

6 tablespoons (¾ stick) unsalted butter
2 eggs
⅓ cup (packed) light brown sugar
1 cup unsweetened applesauce
1½ cups finely chopped mixed dried fruit, such as prunes, figs, apricots, raisins, apples, cranberries, or cherries
1¾ cups all-purpose flour
1 teaspoon baking powder
1 teaspoon baking soda
¼ teaspoon coarse salt
2 teaspoons ground cinnamon
1 teaspoon ground ginger
½ teaspoon ground allspice

1. Preheat the oven to 400° F. Line 8 standard-size muffin cups with paper liners or grease well.

2. In a small saucepan heat the butter over high heat until brown and foamy, watching carefully so it doesn't blacken or burn. Continue heating until the bubbles subside and the butter is dark brown and smoking and gives off a nutty aroma. Pour the butter into a large bowl, whisking constantly, scraping all the brown flecks from the bottom of the pan. Whisk in the eggs, brown sugar, and applesauce. Stir in the dried fruit.

3. In a medium bowl combine the flour, baking powder, soda, salt, cinnamon, ginger, and allspice. With a wooden spoon quickly incorporate the dry ingredients into the applesauce mixture. Fill the muffin cups to the top, mounding slightly.

4. Bake in the top third of the oven for 20 to 22 minutes, until golden brown and crisp on top. Remove from the oven, cool slightly, and remove the muffins from the pan to a rack to cool.

Makes 8 muffins

Sour Cream Corn Muffins

If you add a chopped jalapeño pepper to the batter and sprinkle the tops of the muffins with half a cup of grated white Cheddar cheese, these breakfast muffins can be served with a dinner of grilled ribs or chicken. Make the muffins in summer, when corn is at its sweetest.

2 large ears yellow or white corn (about 2 cups kernels)
1 cup all-purpose flour
1 cup yellow cornmeal
1 tablespoon baking powder
1 teaspoon baking soda
1 teaspoon coarse salt
8 tablespoons (1 stick) unsalted butter, melted
1 cup sour cream
3 tablespoons honey
3 eggs

1. Preheat the oven to 350° F. Grease 10 standard-size muffin cups well or line with paper liners.

2. With a sharp knife scrape the kernels from the corn cobs and place in a food processor fitted with the metal blade. Pulse on and off until finely chopped but not pureed. Transfer to a large mixing bowl and stir together with the flour, cornmeal, baking powder, baking soda, and salt.

3. Make a well in the center of the dry ingredients and pour in the melted butter, sour cream, honey, and eggs. Whisk until well incorporated. Fill the muffin cups to the top with batter.

4. Bake in the upper third of the oven for 20 minutes, or until a toothpick inserted into the center of a muffin comes out clean. Cool muffins in the pan for 5 minutes, then remove to a rack.

Makes 10 muffins

Banana Poppyseed Muffins

Some advance planning is necessary for these muffins because very ripe—black—bananas are essential. Do not use underripe fruit. The poppyseeds mirror the banana's own tiny seeds. One of our children's very favorite muffins.

8 tablespoons (1 stick) unsalted butter, melted and browned
¾ cup (packed) light brown sugar
1¼ cups mashed very ripe (black) bananas (2 or 3 large)
2 eggs
1 cup buttermilk
1⅔ cups cake flour
1 tablespoon baking powder
1 teaspoon baking soda
½ teaspoon coarse salt
3 teaspoons poppyseeds
¾ cup coarsely chopped walnuts, toasted for 10 minutes in a
      350° F. oven

TOPPING
8 thin slices ripe banana
1 teaspoon ground cinnamon mixed with 3 tablespoons
      granulated sugar

1. Preheat the oven to 375° F. Place paper liners in 10 standard-size muffin cups or grease well.

2. In a large mixing bowl whisk together the butter, brown sugar, bananas, eggs, and buttermilk.

3. In another bowl stir together the flour, baking powder, baking soda, salt, and poppyseeds. Add the dry ingredients to the butter mixture and mix well. Fold in the walnuts. Fill the muffin cups to the top. Put a thin slice of banana on each muffin and sprinkle heavily with cinnamon sugar.

4. Bake in the upper third of the oven for 18 to 20 minutes. Remove the muffins from the pan to a cooling rack and serve warm or at room temperature.

Makes 10 muffins

Variation: After the walnuts, fold in ¼ cup coarsely chopped semisweet chocolate or chocolate chips.

Blueberry Muffins with Nutmeg Topping

Everyone loves blueberry muffins, and our family is no exception. The two tablespoons of whole wheat flour give the batter a bit more character, but if you don't have any, go ahead and use more all-purpose.

8 tablespoons (1 stick) unsalted butter,
  at room temperature
½ cup granulated sugar
½ cup confectioners' sugar
1½ tablespoons pure vanilla extract
2 eggs
1 cup buttermilk or plain yogurt
1 teaspoon freshly grated nutmeg
1 tablespoon baking powder
½ teaspoon coarse salt
1⅓ cups cake flour
1 cup all-purpose flour
2 tablespoons whole wheat flour
2 cups fresh blueberries

TOPPING

½ teaspoon freshly grated nutmeg stirred into ⅓ cup
  granulated sugar

1. Preheat the oven to 400° F. Line 10 standard-size muffin cups with paper liners or grease well.

2. In a large mixing bowl cream the butter with both sugars until very light in color. Scrape the sides of the bowl with a rubber spatula and add the vanilla, eggs, and buttermilk, beating constantly.

3. In another bowl stir together the nutmeg, baking powder, salt, and flours. Add to the butter mixture and mix well. Gently fold in the blueberries. Fill muffin cups to the top with batter. Sprinkle each muffin with about 2 teaspoons of nutmeg sugar and place in the upper third of the oven.

4. Bake for 18 to 20 minutes, until the tops are lightly browned. Remove the muffins from the pan to a cooling rack and serve warm or at room temperature.

Makes 10 muffins

Sour Cream Chocolate Muffins

If a chocolate muffin does not appeal to you for breakfast, use these instead of cupcakes for a child's party. Equally good with powdered sugar or iced with your favorite chocolate frosting.

6 ounces unsweetened chocolate
12 tablespoons (1½ sticks) unsalted butter
1 cup water
2 whole eggs
3 egg yolks
1 cup plus 2 tablespoons sugar
1½ teaspoons vanilla extract
⅓ cup sour cream
½ cup cake flour
½ cup all-purpose flour
1½ teaspoons baking soda
¾ teaspoon baking powder

GARNISH
Confectioners' sugar

1. Preheat the oven to 400° F. Line 12 standard-size muffin cups with paper liners or grease well.

2. In the top of a double boiler set over simmering water or in a heavy saucepan over low heat melt together the chocolate, butter, and water. Set aside to cool slightly.

3. In the bowl of an electric mixer on high speed beat the eggs, egg yolks, and sugar until very light in color. On medium speed add the vanilla, sour cream, and chocolate mixture.

4. In another bowl stir together the flours, baking soda, and baking powder. Add to the egg mixture, mixing only enough to moisten.

5. Spoon the batter into a large pastry tube (tip not necessary) and pipe it in swirls, filling the cups to the top and mounding slightly, or spoon the batter in.

6. Bake in the upper third of the oven for 20 minutes. When cool, generously dust the tops with sifted confectioners' sugar.

Makes 12 muffins

Ginger Scones

This rich cream biscuit, studded with chopped candied ginger, is softer and more tender in texture than a traditional scone. We make the scones large and serve them warm with Gingered Pear Marmalade (recipe follows) or another good-quality marmalade.

2¾ cups cake flour
1 teaspoon sugar
4 teaspoons baking powder
12 tablespoons (1½ sticks) unsalted butter, cold
⅓ cup rinsed, dried, and finely chopped candied ginger
1 cup heavy cream

1. Preheat the oven to 400° F.

2. In the bowl of an electric mixer combine the flour, sugar, and baking powder. Cut the butter into tablespoon-size pieces and mix into dry ingredients on low speed with the paddle attachment, or combine by hand with two knives or a pastry blender. The mixture should resemble a fine meal. Stir in the ginger. Pour in the cream and stir or mix just until the dough holds together.

3. Turn the dough out onto a lightly floured surface and knead gently to form a ball. Roll into a ¾-inch-thick circle and cut with a 3-inch biscuit cutter. You should get 7 or 8 scones. Gather the remaining dough together and shape again into a circle, handling as little as possible. Cut out about 3 more scones and place all the scones on a baking sheet. They may be refrigerated for up to 3 hours before baking.

4. Return the scones to room temperature. Bake the scones for 12 to 15 minutes, until the tops are cracked and very light brown. Remove to a wire rack. Serve warm or at room temperature.

Makes 10 or 11 large scones

Variation: Substitute ¼ cup currants and 2 teaspoons finely chopped orange zest for the candied ginger.

Gingered Pear Marmalade

Fresh ginger, fresh pears, dried ginger, and dried pears give this marmalade an intense flavor. Good on scones, muffins, or toast as well as folded into vanilla ice cream. Keeps well in the refrigerator for weeks.

½ cup sugar
2¼ cups water
¼ cup very finely shredded or julienned fresh gingerroot
    (3-inch piece)
4 Bosc pears (about 2 pounds)
2 tablespoons lemon juice
8 dried pear halves
½ cup finely chopped candied ginger
1 tablespoon lime juice

   1. In a medium saucepan bring the sugar and water to a boil. Add the gingerroot and simmer for 10 minutes.

   2. Quarter the pears, cut out the cores, and cut crosswise into ¼-inch slices. Add to the ginger and syrup in the saucepan. Stir in the lemon juice. Cut the dried pears into ¼-inch strips and add to the pan. Cover the pan and simmer over very low heat for about 40 minutes, just until almost all the liquid has been absorbed. Add the candied ginger, cover, and cook over very low heat for 1 hour, stirring occasionally.

   3. Remove from the heat and stir in the lime juice. Cool to room temperature and refrigerate if not using immediately.

Makes 3 cups

Antipasto and Appetizers

The word "antipasto" means "before the pasta" in Italian. Traditionally, Italians liked to have an antipasto, followed by a pasta dish, then the meat main course, a vegetable, and dessert. Most modern Italians don't eat that much food at one meal, and they are much more flexible about the order than in the past. Regardless of how it is served, an antipasto platter is colorful, artful, and a real crowd-pleaser. It can be as simple or as complex as you like, for there are literally hundreds of combinations of ingredients that go together beautifully. The only real rule is to make sure that not everything on the platter is very acidic, even if you love strong vinaigrettes (as we do). You need something slightly sweet, something salty—like prosciutto, salami, or olives—and something sour or pungent. Some offerings should be warm, some cold. And we like to put something fresh, like tufts of arugula, frisée, or chicory, along the edge of the platter. In other words, the flavors and textures need to be balanced. The wonderful thing about an antipasto platter is that there is something for everyone. Guests can nibble a little, drift away, and then come back to the platter later, making it ideal for casual entertaining.

To serve four people, no more than four items are necessary— perhaps the Fennel and Onion Salad or Sweet-and-Sour Spring Onions, a good purchased salami, a cheese like ricotta salata, and tender Grilled Asparagus.

When we have eight friends over, we have five or six items arranged for balance and interest on two platters. These might include toasted slices of baguette accompanying Roasted Eggplant and Red Peppers, Chicken Liver Spread, and Tuna Tartare, all served in ramekins; Braised Artichokes; Marinated Mushrooms; and little goat-cheese *crottins*. Other good cheeses for an antipasto platter are buffalo mozzarella, pecorino, and taleggio.

We both grew up in the fifties, when the relish tray for company included carrot and celery sticks, radishes, and black olives. Period. Think how much more visually exciting and intensely flavored an anti-pasto platter can be today. Most of the recipes in this chapter can be prepared ahead and refrigerated until serving. With a spectacular anti-pasto platter in the center of the table and a big bowl of pasta waiting in the kitchen, it's a party.

Braised Artichokes

The artichoke is a member of the thistle family, which accounts for the prickly choke at its center. Select very small artichokes; there will be less choke, and the whole vegetable is apt to be more tender. Leave some of the stem attached. With a light wine sauce, the artichokes can be part of a luncheon menu as well as an antipasto platter. Allow one artichoke per person for a side dish, and half of one for a buffet.

4 small heavy artichokes (6 ounces each)
3 tablespoons lemon juice
4 tablespoons olive oil
4 tablespoons chopped shallots
1 teaspoon chopped fresh thyme or ½ teaspoon dried thyme
1 teaspoon chopped fresh marjoram or ½ teaspoon dried marjoram
3 garlic cloves, finely chopped
1 cup white wine
1½ cups chicken broth, preferably homemade (page 75)
¼ teaspoon coarse salt
¼ teaspoon coarsely ground black pepper
½ cup finely chopped fresh chervil or flat-leaf parsley

1. Cut off the bottom 5 rows of leaves of each artichoke. Then cut off the top ½ inch from the remaining leaves to remove the sharp spines. Pare off the outer fibrous layer of the stems. Cut artichokes in half through the stem and place in a bowl of water to which 2 tablespoons of the lemon juice has been added.

2. Heat 1 tablespoon of the olive oil in a large skillet over high heat. Remove the artichokes from the water and pat dry with a towel. Place cut side down in the skillet and sauté, without turning, until lightly browned. Add 2 tablespoons of the shallots and the thyme, marjoram, garlic, wine, broth, salt, and pepper and bring to a boil. Cover the skillet, reduce the heat, and cook for 20 minutes, until the artichokes are tender when pierced with the tip of a knife. Remove the artichokes to a plate.

3. Turn the heat up to high, and continue cooking the sauce until reduced to ½ cup. Add the remaining shallots, lemon juice, and olive oil. Simmer for 2 to 3 minutes and remove from the heat.

4. Scoop out the choke and small inner leaves of the artichokes. Pour some sauce over each half, garnish with finely chopped chervil or Italian parsley, and serve. If not serving immediately, refrigerate the artichokes and sauce separately for as long as overnight. Allow to come to room temperature before serving. Gently squeeze each artichoke half to remove any accumulated liquid before saucing.

Serves 8 as part of a 5- or 6-dish antipasto platter or 4 as a side dish

Grilled Asparagus

For grilling you need large, thick asparagus, not the very thin, "pencil" asparagus. Look at the tips to make sure the asparagus hasn't begun to flower. Blanching the asparagus with a quick dip in boiling salted water softens the stalks just enough for them to be pierced by the skewers without breaking; it also reduces the grilling time. It is easier to support and turn the asparagus if you use two skewers. If using bamboo skewers, soak them in water for half an hour before grilling to avoid burning.

12 thick stalks asparagus (about 1¼ pounds)
Olive oil
Coarse salt

VINAIGRETTE
3 tablespoons extra-virgin olive oil
1 tablespoon lemon juice
2 teaspoons finely chopped shallots
¼ teaspoon coarse salt
Coarsely ground black pepper
½ cup fresh bread crumbs, toasted in a 350° F. oven until
crisp (about 5 minutes)

1. Prepare a barbecue grill.
2. Trim 1 to 2 inches off the large end of each asparagus or cut all the asparagus to 6 inches. Lightly peel the lower half to remove the thin outer layer of skin. Drop the asparagus into boiling salted water and boil for 1 minute. Drain and plunge into ice water for 2 to 3 minutes.

3. Remove the asparagus from the water and lay 4 pieces close together, all in the same direction. Insert 2 skewers through all 4 stalks, a third of the way from each end, leaving a ½-inch space between the stalks. Repeat with the remaining asparagus. Brush with olive oil and sprinkle with salt.

4. Grill over hot coals, turning once, just long enough to color lightly and warm throughout, about 1½ minutes on each side.

5. To make the vinaigrette, stir together the olive oil, lemon juice, shallots, salt, and a few grindings of pepper. Arrange the asparagus on a serving platter and spoon the vinaigrette on top. Sprinkle with toasted bread crumbs and serve.

Serves 6 as part of a 4-dish antipasto platter or 4 as a side dish

Marinated Mushrooms

Although different kinds of mushrooms may be used in this dish, we generally use the white button kind about the size of a quarter. They should be firm, white, and tightly closed beneath the cap.

1 pound medium white mushrooms, wiped clean and left whole
4 tablespoons olive oil
3 garlic cloves, minced
¼ cup balsamic vinegar
½ medium onion, very thinly sliced
2 tablespoons chopped fresh tarragon or 2 teaspoons dried
     tarragon
¼ teaspoon coarse salt
¼ teaspoon coarsely ground black pepper

GARNISH
1 tablespoon chopped fresh chives
1 tablespoon chopped fresh flat-leaf parsley

1. In a large skillet over medium heat toss together the mushrooms and 2 tablespoons of the olive oil. Sauté until the mushrooms have shrunk about a quarter in size and have darkened. Transfer from the pan to a bowl.

2. Add the garlic and vinegar to the skillet and cook, stirring, over medium heat until the garlic has softened. Add the onion, the remaining olive oil, and the tarragon, salt, and pepper and stir together for 3 minutes. Remove the skillet from the heat and cool to room temperature. (It's important to do this because hot marinade would cause the mushrooms to cook further and give off more juices.) When the marinade has cooled, toss with the mushrooms, cover, and refrigerate until needed. The dish will keep for about 3 days.

3. Before serving, taste and adjust the seasonings if necessary. Sprinkle with chives and parsley.

Serves 6 as a part of a 4-dish antipasto platter

Sweet-and-Sour
Spring Onions

This piquant appetizer is what the Italians call agrodolce *(sour-sweet). If you can find real spring onions, use them. They are tender and hold together well. Shaped like a scallion but with a rounder end, this purple-tinged early spring vegetable also makes a beautiful presentation. Tiny boiling onions can also be used.*

1 pound spring onions or tiny boiling onions
2 tablespoons olive oil
¼ teaspoon coarse salt
¼ teaspoon coarsely ground black pepper
¼ cup red wine
¼ cup balsamic vinegar
½ cup chopped fresh flat-leaf parsley

1. Remove the root ends and green tops from spring onions. If using boiling onions, remove the root ends and peel off the papery layers of skin.

2. In a large skillet heat the olive oil. Spread out the onions in a single layer, toss with salt and pepper, and sauté over high heat until lightly browned. Pour in the wine and vinegar, cover the pan, lower the heat, and simmer for 10 minutes. Uncover the pan and raise the heat to high. Cook, turning the onions, until the sauce is syrupy and coats the onions, about 3 minutes. Pour into a bowl and refrigerate, covered, for several hours or as long as 3 days.

3. Before serving, taste and adjust the seasonings if necessary and sprinkle with parsley.

Serves 6 to 8 as part of a 5- or 6-dish antipasto platter

Fennel and Onion Salad

Make this in winter or early spring, when fennel is younger, rounder, and less stringy. Flat, skinny bulbs are not very tender or flavorful. This is a variation on onion salad, with the fennel adding sweetness and substance. It is delicious served with swordfish or a roasted whole fish. It is the perfect relish for a prosciutto sandwich (page 136).

2 large fennel bulbs (about 1 pound each)
1 red onion, sliced paper thin
3 tablespoons lemon juice
4 tablespoons extra-virgin olive oil
½ teaspoon coarse salt
½ teaspoon coarsely ground black pepper

1. Trim the feathery greens from the fennel bulbs and reserve. Cut off the stalks and discard. Cut in half through the stem end and place cut side down on a cutting board. Slice very thin, keeping the layers together. Place the fennel and onion slices in a colander and rinse for several minutes with very cold water. Dry in a salad spinner or blot dry.

2. Put the slices in a bowl and toss with 2 tablespoons of the lemon juice, 3 tablespoons of the olive oil, and the salt and pepper.

3. Pull off the leaves of the reserved fennel greens and add about half of them to the salad. Toss to combine. Let stand for 10 minutes, then sprinkle with the remaining lemon juice and olive oil and toss again. Cover and refrigerate if not using immediately. The salad will keep for about 2 days.

Serves 6 to 8 as part of a 5- or 6-dish antipasto platter or 6 as a salad

Roasted Eggplant and Red Peppers

If you can't fire up the barbecue, you can broil the eggplant and peppers. Keep them far enough away from the heat for the skins to char slowly. This slow charring imparts the smoky taste that is so delicious. Spread on a crostini of French or country bread, this mixture makes a perfect appetizer.

2 large eggplants (1½ pounds each)
1 red bell pepper
¼ cup pitted and finely chopped kalamata olives
2 tablespoons balsamic vinegar
2 tablespoons chopped fresh flat-leaf parsley
2 tablespoons extra-virgin olive oil
Coarse salt
Coarsely ground black pepper

1. Prepare a barbecue grill or preheat the broiler.

2. Place the eggplants and pepper directly on a barbecue grate over hot coals or on a rack on a baking sheet about 4 inches from the broiler unit. Char on all sides, turning to cook evenly. Grill the eggplant until very soft and completely blackened, about 30 minutes.

3. Place the pepper in a plastic bag to steam while preparing the eggplants. Cut the eggplants in half lengthwise through the stem end and carefully pull out the seeds. Scrape all the pulp from the skin and put the pulp in a colander. Drain for 30 minutes.

4. Cut the pepper in half, remove the stem and seeds, and carefully peel off the blackened skin (see Note). Finely chop the pepper and set aside in a medium bowl.

5. Press out any excess liquid from the eggplant pulp, finely chop it, and add it to the bowl with the pepper. Stir in the olives, vinegar, parsley, olive oil, and salt and pepper to taste. Serve immediately or refrigerate and bring to room temperature before serving.

Serves 8 to 10 as part of a 5- or 6-dish antipasto platter or 5 or 6 as a side dish

Note: Don't be tempted to rinse the peppers under running water; it will make them soggy and the mixture too liquid.

Roasted Red and Yellow Peppers

Sometimes grilling peppers until they are charred and tender seems tedious—and you still have to create a marinade to flavor them. But if they are lightly grilled, then baked, the pepper juices are the sauce. Don't be put off by the three cooking methods here; the time goes very fast.

2 large red bell peppers
2 yellow bell peppers
3 garlic cloves, finely chopped
1 teaspoon finely chopped fresh thyme or ½ teaspoon dried thyme
2 teaspoons finely chopped fresh flat-leaf parsley
½ teaspoon coarse salt
¼ teaspoon coarsely ground black pepper
2 tablespoons olive oil
2 tablespoons capers

1. Prepare a barbecue grill. Preheat the oven to 400° F.

2. Quarter the peppers through the stem end and remove the seeds and ribs. Grill 5 minutes over hot coals, just until the peppers become a mottled black color. Remove the peppers from the grill and place them on a large sheet of aluminum foil.

3. Sprinkle the peppers with the garlic, thyme, parsley, salt, pepper, and oil. Wrap tightly and put on a cookie sheet in the center of the oven. Bake for 15 minutes and place in a bowl.

4. Pour the juices and seasonings into a small skillet and boil over high heat until the juices have been reduced by half. Pour over the peppers and toss in a bowl with the capers. Chill.

Serves 6 as part of a 4-dish antipasto platter

Tapenade

Tapenade is an olive paste that probably originated in Provence. We make it with Greek kalamata olives, which are larger and easier to pit than the French niçoise olives. This is a powerfully flavored condiment that has many uses—on crostini, in Rare Tuna Salade Niçoise (page 119), with pasta, or on pizza crust. If you use the Tapenade as an appetizer spread, combine it with half a cup of finely diced tomatoes to diffuse the intensity.

One 8.5-ounce jar or can kalamata olives
3 garlic cloves, thinly sliced
½ teaspoon grated lemon zest
2 anchovy fillets
2 teaspoons lemon juice
¼ teaspoon coarsely ground black pepper
⅓ cup extra-virgin olive oil

1. Drain the olives and gently press with a rolling pin to crush slightly. This will make them easier to pit. Remove the pits and reserve. Place the olives in a food processor fitted with the metal blade. Add the garlic, lemon zest, anchovies, lemon juice, and pepper. Pulse on and off to make a coarse puree.

2. In a small saucepan heat the olive oil with the olive pits and simmer over low heat for 3 to 4 minutes. Pour the oil through a strainer into the processor and pulse to combine with the olive puree. Serve immediately or refrigerate for up to 1 week. Bring to room temperature and stir before serving.

Serves 8 as part of a 6-dish antipasto platter

Squid and Orecchiette

Orecchiette means "little ears," and the shape of this dried pasta is perfect for catching sauce. When the pasta is combined with tender white rings of squid, the dish becomes a tantalizing appetizer or antipasto offering. Begin one day ahead to infuse the almond oil; other than that, the recipe goes together quickly and easily.

2 cups almond or light vegetable oil
2 lemons, cut in half
1 bay leaf
1 small dried red chili or ¼ teaspoon crushed red pepper
½ pound dried orecchiette
1 tablespoon olive oil
1 pound cleaned small squid, cut into ⅛-inch rings (2 pounds
     before cleaning)
½ red onion, finely chopped
1 garlic clove, minced
¼ cup lemon juice
½ teaspoon coarse salt
¼ teaspoon coarsely ground black pepper
¼ cup chopped fresh chives

1. In a small saucepan heat the almond oil with the lemons, bay leaf, and chili. Heat until very hot without boiling, then remove from the heat and allow to stand for 2 days. Strain.

2. Bring a large pot of salted water to a boil and simmer the pasta over medium-low heat until completely done, about 12 minutes. (If orecchiette is cooked over high heat, the pasta is apt to break apart before cooking in the center.) Drain well and pour into a bowl. Toss with olive oil. Set aside.

3. Bring more salted water to a boil in the same large pot and blanch the squid for 1 to 2 minutes, until not quite opaque. (They will continue to "cook" in the vinaigrette because of the lemon juice.) Remove with a strainer or slotted spoon and add to the pasta.

4. In a small bowl whisk ½ cup of the flavored oil (reserve the rest for another time) with the onion, garlic, lemon juice, salt, and pepper. Pour over the squid and pasta and toss carefully. Sprinkle with chopped chives. Serve immediately or refrigerate for up to 3 days.

Serves 6 to 8 as part of a 5- or 6-dish antipasto platter or 4 as an appetizer

Tuna Tartare

Use the best deep-red-fleshed tuna you can find, often called "sashimi grade." The tartare is ideal for an antipasto platter. It also makes a delicious hors d'oeuvre spread on a toasted slice of baguette.

½ pound sashimi-grade tuna, ½ inch thick
Coarsely ground black pepper
½ medium red bell pepper, cut into ¼-inch dice
½ yellow bell pepper, cut into ¼-inch dice
2 tablespoons finely chopped red onion
3 tablespoons lemon juice
4 tablespoons olive oil
2 tablespoons chopped fresh flat-leaf parsley
¼ cup finely chopped pitted kalamata olives

1. Prepare a barbecue grill or preheat a cast-iron skillet.

2. Sprinkle ½ teaspoon of ground black pepper evenly over both sides of the tuna. Grill over hot coals just long enough to sear the outside or place in a very hot cast-iron skillet and cook just until the outside turns gray. Remove and cut into ¼-inch dice.

3. Stir together the tuna, peppers, onion, lemon juice, olive oil, parsley, and olives. Season to taste with black pepper. Serve immediately or refrigerate for up to 1 day.

Serves 4 as an appetizer or 6 as part of a 6-dish antipasto platter

Salmon Carpaccio

It goes without saying that you must always use the freshest possible fish, but this is especially true when the fish is served raw. Lightly toasted quarter-inch slices of French baguette are nice with the carpaccio.

½ pound salmon fillet, skin on
5 tablespoons olive oil
4 teaspoons fresh lime juice
1 tablespoon chopped fresh mint
1 tablespoon chopped fresh flat-leaf parsley
1 shallot, thinly sliced
Coarsely ground black pepper

1. Holding a very sharp knife at an angle, cut 8 very thin slices of salmon from the center of the fillet. Place 4 slices on a lightly oiled sheet of plastic wrap, sprinkle with oil, and cover with another sheet of plastic. With the flat side of a meat tenderizer or pounder, pound the salmon pieces until they are half again as large and are translucent, being careful not to tear the fish. Repeat with the remaining 4 slices. Refrigerate if not serving immediately.

2. Thirty minutes or so before serving, cut between the fillets with scissors and remove the top layer of plastic wrap. Allowing 2 pieces per serving, flip the salmon over onto serving plates and carefully peel off the remaining plastic. Drizzle 1 tablespoon of olive oil over each serving, sprinkle with lime juice, and marinate for 30 minutes, covered with plastic wrap.

3. Just before serving, remove the plastic and garnish with mint, parsley, shallots, and a few grindings of black pepper.

Serves 4 as an appetizer

Chicken Liver Spread

This mixture is lighter in texture and a bit coarser than a traditional pâté. For an excellent appetizer we like to fill ramekins with this, Tuna Tartare (page 68), and Roasted Eggplant and Red Peppers (page 62) and serve them with lightly toasted quarter-inch slices of baguette. The tastes are diverse and interesting, and all the spreads can be prepared ahead.

2 tablespoons olive oil
1 tablespoon diced pancetta or bacon
3 tablespoons chopped shallots
1 garlic clove, minced
6 large chicken livers (about ½ pound)
1 teaspoon finely chopped lemon zest
1 teaspoon finely chopped fresh rosemary or ½ teaspoon dried
   rosemary
1 teaspoon finely chopped fresh thyme or ½ teaspoon dried
   thyme
1 tablespoon capers, rinsed and drained
1 tablespoon balsamic vinegar
¼ teaspoon coarse salt
¼ teaspoon coarsely ground black pepper

1. Heat the oil in a medium skillet over medium heat. Stir in the pancetta, shallots, and garlic. Sauté for 2 to 3 minutes. Add the chicken livers and cook for 2 to 3 minutes. Stir in the lemon zest, rosemary, thyme, capers, vinegar, salt, and pepper. Continue cooking until the vinegar is reduced and the livers are done but still barely pink inside, about 5 minutes. Remove from the heat and let cool.

2. Remove the livers and capers with a slotted spoon and chop fine. Stir back into the pan and add a little olive oil if the mixture appears too dry. Taste and adjust the seasoning.

3. Pack into a 1-cup ramekin and serve. If not serving immediately, cover and refrigerate for several hours. Let the spread come back to room temperature before serving.

Serves 6 as part of a 5- or 6-dish antipasto platter or 4 as an appetizer

Arancine

Arancine make a delicious little snack that we love to prepare from leftover risotto. We serve them as part of an antipasto or as an appetizer. Since measurements depend on the amount of risotto you have, exact amounts cannot be given. Allow two or three arancine per person.

Swiss or Fontina cheese
Unseasoned bread crumbs
Oil, preferably peanut oil, for frying

    1. Form cold risotto (page 178) into 1-inch balls. Cut Swiss or fontina cheese into ½-inch cubes and tuck one inside each ball. Roll the balls in unseasoned bread crumbs. The balls can be refrigerated until ready to cook or deep-fried immediately.

    2. Heat 2 inches of oil to 375° F. Drop several balls at a time into the oil without crowding. When the balls are well browned, remove them with a slotted spoon and drain on paper towels.

Soups

There has always been something soul-satisfying about making a pot of soup. More important for a busy working couple is the peace of mind that results from the knowledge that a nutritious, lowfat, delicious "instant" dinner is waiting in the refrigerator, ready to be heated up and served.

Soup offers tremendous flexibility to the cook. It can fit comfortably into any course of a meal or be a balanced meal in itself. Chilled Summer Vegetable Soup might begin an outdoor barbecue, while White Bean Soup is hearty enough to need only a salad and a crusty baguette for a winter supper. Roasted Red Pepper Soup could be the focus of a summer luncheon or a savory starter for an elegant dinner. Very Tomato Soup with Pasta Stars appeals to children (it's Vanessa and Ben's favorite soup), but the flavors are rich and complex enough to make it as suitable for company as for family dinners.

We use—and would urge you to use—only homemade chicken broth when it is called for in a recipe. Chicken broth is very easy to make, and we give a recipe for it in this chapter. It is the most versatile of all the stocks. We have not included a recipe for beef broth because it is much more complicated to make, involving browning bones and roasting vegetables, and we assume that most home cooks don't have the time to devote to it. Besides, chicken broth can often be substituted for beef broth in a red meat sauce; the result will be lighter but equally flavorful.

All of the recipes in this chapter have also been tested with low-salt canned broth, and the results were satisfactory. Try out different brands of canned broth to find out which you prefer, but do avoid the cubes. Canned broth has better flavor and fewer preservatives.

Soups (and chicken stock) are easiest made on the weekend, when the cooking can be done in a leisurely fashion, even in stages if we're really busy. The flavor of most soups improves greatly when they rest in the refrigerator for a day and are reheated, another reason soup-making is an ideal weekend project.

Soup, salad, and bread are a classic combination. We hope that the salad recipes on pages 95–121 will give you some fresh ideas, but the truth of the matter is, all you really need to turn any of these soups into a wonderful meal is the simplest green salad and a chewy loaf of peasant bread.

Homemade Chicken Broth

We prefer to cook with homemade chicken broth. First, the flavor is superior to anything you can buy, and second, if you add a whole chicken to the pot along with the necks and backs, you automatically have cooked chicken for sandwiches or salad. By sautéing the vegetables first, you allow them to release their own flavors before the chicken is added. Chinese markets and some supermarkets sell chicken feet, which are a wonderful addition to chicken stock. Don't hesitate to add them if available.

2 onions, peeled and cut into eighths
2 celery stalks, cut into 1-inch pieces
2 carrots, cut into 1-inch chunks
2 tablespoons safflower oil
¼ cup flat-leaf parsley sprigs
1 garlic head, unpeeled and cut in half horizontally
2 bay leaves
1 tablespoon dried thyme
1 tablespoon whole black peppercorns
1 teaspoon coarse salt
5 pounds chicken backs, necks, and feet, if available
One 3½-pound chicken (optional)
8 quarts water

1. In a very large stockpot over medium heat sauté the onions, celery, and carrots in oil for 10 minutes, until softened. Add the parsley, garlic, bay leaves, thyme, peppercorns, salt, chicken parts, and whole chicken, if using. Pour in the water. Bring to a boil over high heat, reduce to a simmer, and skim any foam that collects on top. Cook, partly covered, for 5 to 6 hours without stirring. If you have added a whole chicken, remove it after 1 hour 30 minutes.

2. Strain the broth through a fine-mesh sieve into containers and cool to room temperature. Cover and refrigerate overnight. Remove the fat when you are ready to use the broth. It may be frozen for up to 1 month.

Makes 5 quarts

Roasted Red Pepper Soup

Deeply colored and distinctly flavored, roasted red pepper puree is very useful to have on hand in the refrigerator. You can add it to salad dressing and cream sauce, or serve it with grilled fish or chicken. Or, as here, you can mix it with chicken broth and water to make a cold summer soup. If you want to serve it hot, warm it slowly over medium heat and stir in more chicken broth until it's as thick as you want it.

4 large red bell peppers
1 large onion, coarsely chopped
3 garlic cloves, cut into thirds
¼ teaspoon crushed red pepper
½ serrano or jalapeño chili, seeded and minced
1 teaspoon coarse salt
1 teaspoon coarsely ground black pepper
3 tablespoons olive oil
1¼ cups chicken broth, preferably homemade (page 75)
¼ cup water
½ cup heavy cream

GARNISH
¼ cup finely chopped chives

1. Preheat the oven to 400° F.
2. Place two 24-inch-long sheets of aluminum foil perpendicular to each other on a cookie sheet with centers overlapping. Place the peppers and onion on the foil, sprinkle with garlic, crushed pepper, fresh chili, salt, and pepper, and drizzle with olive oil. Wrap securely so that no juices will escape and place the cookie sheet in the upper third of the oven. Bake for 1 hour.
3. Remove from the oven and let cool without opening the foil. When cool enough to handle, remove the skin from the peppers, cut them in half, and scrape the seeds and core from the inside.
4. Place the roasted peppers and vegetables, along with any liquid that has accumulated in the foil, in a food processor fitted with the metal blade. Puree until smooth. Add the chicken broth and water and pulse until combined. Pour into a nonreactive bowl, cover, and refrigerate for several hours or as long as overnight.

5. When ready to serve, whisk the cream in a medium bowl just until airy and light. Ladle the soup into 6 bowls and carefully float 2 tablespoons of cream in the center of each. Sprinkle with chives and serve.

Serves **6**

Warm Leek and Potato Soup

A good leek and potato soup should be simple enough to make in one pot, and to make fast. This soup can be prepared ahead and reheated.

4 large leeks
4 tablespoons (½ stick) unsalted butter
2 teaspoons coarse salt
1 pound russet potatoes, peeled and cut into 1-inch dice
1 cup chicken broth, preferably homemade (page 75)
1 bay leaf
3 thyme sprigs or ½ teaspoon dried thyme
2½ cups half-and-half or light cream
1½ cups water

GARNISH
2 scallions, green parts only, finely chopped, or 2 tablespoons
**   finely chopped fresh chives**

1. Trim off the roots and half the green part of the leeks and cut in half lengthwise. Cut into ½-inch pieces, place in a colander, and rinse well.

2. In a large saucepan or soup pot over low heat melt 3 tablespoons of the butter and sauté the leeks with 1 teaspoon of the salt until wilted. Add the potatoes and stir in the chicken broth, bay leaf, thyme, half-and-half, water, and remaining 1 teaspoon of salt. Simmer slowly, uncovered, for 15 to 20 minutes, until the potatoes are tender. Do not boil.

3. Place a strainer over a large bowl and pour the soup through. Spoon the vegetables into a food processor fitted with the metal blade and pulse to make a chunky puree.

4. Return the mixture to the pot, add the soup liquid and more water if needed, and warm over low heat.

5. Stir in the remaining 1 tablespoon of butter before serving. Garnish with finely chopped scallions or chives.

Serves 6

Hearty Mushroom Soup

This soup has an intense earthy flavor that is subtly altered by the kind of mushrooms you choose for it. We sometimes substitute fresh shiitake mushrooms for some of the white ones.

½ ounce dried shiitake mushrooms, broken up
½ ounce other dried mushrooms, such as porcini or
    chanterelles, or more shiitakes, unsoaked
3 tablespoons unsalted butter
3 tablespoons flour
1 small onion, finely chopped
4 garlic cloves, minced
1½ pounds medium white mushrooms, thinly sliced
½ teaspoon coarse salt
¼ teaspoon coarsely ground black pepper
1 teaspoon dried thyme
½ teaspoon dried marjoram
4 cups beef broth
4 cups water

GARNISH
3 tablespoons chopped fresh chives

1. Soak the dried mushrooms in ¼ cup water. Pour off and discard the sand. Set the mushrooms aside.

2. In a heavy soup pot melt the butter over medium heat and stir in the flour to make a smooth paste. Add the onion, garlic, and fresh mushrooms and cook until the mushrooms release their liquid. Turn the heat to low and stir in the salt, pepper, dried mushrooms, thyme, and marjoram. Cook until all the mushrooms are soft and wilted, stirring often.

3. Add the broth and water. Simmer, covered, for 1 hour 30 minutes, until all the mushrooms are very tender.

4. Ladle into soup bowls and garnish each with a sprinkling of chives.

Serves 6

Note: Can be made 1 to 2 days ahead and reheated over low heat.

Very Tomato Soup with Pasta Stars

This soup combines three kinds of tomatoes, or rather tomatoes in three different states: fresh, canned, and dried. Cook the pasta stars separately so you can tell the minute they're done; overcooked pasta will make the soup too thick. Garnish the soup with chopped parsley or crumbled bacon and serve it with a large garlic crouton. Your kids will love it—ours do.

1 small onion, finely chopped
4 tablespoons olive oil
3 large garlic cloves
½ teaspoon dried tarragon
½ teaspoon dried thyme
One 28-ounce can peeled tomatoes with liquid
7 very ripe medium tomatoes, cored, peeled, seeded, and
    chopped (3½ to 4 pounds)
8 sun-dried tomatoes or Oven-dried Tomatoes (page 99), finely
    chopped
2 cups chicken broth, preferably homemade (page 75)
1½ cups water
2 teaspoons coarse salt
1 teaspoon coarsely ground black pepper
4 teaspoons sugar
½ cup dried pasta stars or other very small pasta

GARNISH (OPTIONAL)
Chopped fresh flat-leaf parsley or crumbled bacon

1. In a large soup pot over medium heat sauté the onion in olive oil
until soft. Stir in the garlic, tarragon, thyme, canned tomatoes, three-
quarters of the fresh tomatoes, the sun-dried tomatoes, the broth, and
1 cup of water. Cover and simmer for 1 hour 30 minutes, until the
mixture has thickened and the tomatoes are very soft.

2. Place a colander over a large bowl and pour the soup through. Return 1 cup of the solids in the colander to the pot and puree the remainder in a food processor fitted with the metal blade. Return the puree with the remaining liquid to the pot. Stir in the salt, pepper, sugar, and remaining ½ cup of water. Cover and simmer over low heat for 15 minutes to blend the flavors. Remove from the heat.

3. In a separate pot filled with boiling salted water, cook the pasta stars just until barely done. Drain and add to the soup. Stir in the remaining chopped fresh tomatoes.

4. Ladle into soup bowls and garnish with parsley or bacon if desired.

Serves 6

White Bean Soup

White beans can be turned into many delicious, nutritious, and economical dishes. In this recipe they are simmered with seasonings in a rich chicken broth, then pureed to make a very satisfying winter soup. We also enjoy this hearty soup on cool foggy days in May and June in California.

1 pound Great Northern white beans
1 tablespoon olive oil
1 small onion, finely chopped
2 cups chicken broth, preferably homemade (page 75)
8 cups water
¾ pound smoked ham hock
2 garlic cloves
1 teaspoon fresh thyme or ½ teaspoon dried thyme
1 bay leaf
1¼ teaspoons coarsely ground black pepper
1 teaspoon coarse salt

GARNISH
2 tomatoes, seeded and diced
2 teaspoons chopped fresh thyme

1. Rinse the beans in several changes of water, cover with fresh water, and soak overnight.

2. The next day, heat the olive oil in a soup pot and sauté the onion over medium heat until soft. Drain the beans and measure out 3 cups. Add to the onion. Pour in the broth and water. Add the ham hock, garlic, thyme, bay leaf, and pepper. Cover and simmer for 1 hour 30 minutes, until the beans are soft. Discard the bay leaf.

3. With a slotted spoon transfer all the solid ingredients except the ham hock and 2 cups of beans to a food processor fitted with the metal blade and puree. Return this puree to the pot with the liquid and stir.

Add the remaining soaked beans with the ham hock. Cook for ½ hour, until the soup has thickened and all the beans are tender. Remove the ham hock, slit the skin, pull the meat from the bone, and add the meat to the soup. Season with salt and more pepper if needed.

4. Ladle into soup bowls and top with tomatoes and thyme.

Serves 6 to 8

Onion Soup with Whole Glazed Shallots

For best flavor, the onions for this soup must be cooked down very slowly to a deep brown color. This is best done in a deep, heavy-bottomed soup pot. Stir often to prevent burning.

3 pounds white onions, peeled and thinly sliced
¼ cup olive oil
Coarse salt
Coarsely ground black pepper
2 cups dry sherry
¼ cup red wine vinegar
1 bay leaf
2 thyme sprigs or ½ teaspoon dried thyme
4 cups beef broth
2½ cups water

CROUTONS
6 slices French bread, cut ¼ inch thick on the diagonal
3 tablespoons olive oil
6 tablespoons grated parmesan cheese

12 Glazed Shallots (page 231)

1. Place the onions, olive oil, ½ teaspoon salt, and ¼ teaspoon pepper in a soup pot and stir to combine. Cook over low heat, stirring often, until all the moisture from the onions has evaporated and they have turned brown. This will take about 30 to 40 minutes.

2. Add the sherry, vinegar, bay leaf, thyme, broth, and water. Taste and add more salt and pepper if needed. Simmer, covered, for 1 hour 30 minutes. Remove the bay leaf and thyme sprigs.

3. To make the croutons, drizzle some olive oil over each slice of bread and broil until lightly browned. Sprinkle with parmesan and place under the broiler until the cheese is golden brown.

4. To serve, place 2 shallots in each of 6 bowls and ladle in the soup. Float a crouton on top.

Serves 6

Very Celery Soup

In this soup celery stalks, root, and leaves are all simmered together. The potato adds mellowness. Hearty, full of celery flavor, and thickened with vegetable puree, this soup could be accented with a dollop of Crème Fraîche (page 248) or sour cream.

3 tablespoons unsalted butter
1 small onion, finely chopped
1 garlic clove
2 leeks, washed well and sliced ¼ inch thick
4 celery stalks, including leaves, cut into ¼-inch pieces
3 medium red potatoes, peeled and coarsely chopped (about
    1½ pounds)
¾ pound celery root, peeled and cut into ½-inch dice, leaves
    reserved
1 teaspoon coarse salt
¼ teaspoon coarsely ground black pepper
2 cups chicken broth, preferably homemade (page 75)
4 cups water
½ lemon

1. In a soup pot melt the butter over very low heat. Add the onion, garlic, and leeks and all but ¼ cup of the celery. Cook, stirring occasionally, until the vegetables are softened, about 20 minutes. Add all but ½ cup of the potatoes and the celery root, salt, and pepper. Cook, stirring, until all the vegetables are soft, taking care not to brown them. Stir in the broth and water, cover, and simmer for 30 minutes.

2. Transfer the vegetables to a food processor fitted with the metal blade. Pulse and return to the pot with the liquid and stir to incorporate.

3. Place a large coarse-mesh strainer or a colander over another pot and pour the soup through. With the back of a spoon, press the solids through the strainer. Bring to a boil and add the reserved ¼ cup chopped celery and ½ cup chopped potato. Simmer until these vegetables are tender.

4. To serve, ladle into soup bowls, sprinkle with chopped celery-root leaves, and squeeze some lemon juice over the soup.

Serves 4 to 6

Note: May be made early in the day and reheated to serve at dinner.

Chilled Summer Vegetable Soup

A rich soup can be made with just vegetables, without any meat broth at all. Because this soup is best chilled, add the cool sautéed spinach right before serving.

PUREE

¼ cup olive oil
½ onion, coarsely chopped
1 red bell pepper, seeded and cut into ½-inch dice
¼ teaspoon crushed red pepper
4 large garlic cloves, minced
2 flat-leaf parsley sprigs
2 celery stalks, chopped
2 carrots, peeled and chopped
2 medium zucchini, cut into ½-inch pieces
3 oregano sprigs, rubbed between hands
10 Italian plum tomatoes, seeded and chopped
One 14½-ounce can whole tomatoes with liquid
1 teaspoon coarse salt

2 tablespoons olive oil
½ onion, finely chopped
½ red bell pepper, seeded and finely chopped
2 small carrots, peeled and finely chopped
½ pound green beans, strings and ends removed and finely
    chopped
1½ cups diced zucchini
4 Italian plum tomatoes
Coarse salt

¾ pound fresh spinach, washed and stems removed
2 tablespoons olive oil
3 cups water
¼ teaspoon coarsely ground black pepper
¼ teaspoon cayenne
4 teaspoons extra-virgin olive oil

1. For the soup puree, in a large skillet heat ¼ cup of the olive oil over medium heat. Add the onion, bell pepper, crushed pepper, garlic, parsley, celery, carrots, zucchini, and oregano. Cover and sweat the vegetables over low heat for 1 hour, stirring occasionally. Add the fresh and canned tomatoes and stir.

2. Transfer the vegetables in batches to a food processor fitted with the metal blade and puree. Place a strainer over a soup pot and pour in any liquid left in the skillet and half of the pureed vegetables. Press the puree through the strainer into the pot. Repeat with the remaining puree, scraping the bottom of the strainer often. Discard the solids remaining in the strainer. Place the soup pot over low heat.

3. To cook the soup vegetables, in the same skillet heat 2 tablespoons of olive oil over medium heat. Add the onion, bell pepper, carrots, green beans, and zucchini. Sauté for 10 minutes, then add the tomatoes and salt to taste. When the vegetables are crisp-tender, remove them from the skillet and add to the liquid in the soup pot. Cook over low heat for 30 minutes to blend the flavors. Remove from the heat, cool to room temperature, and refrigerate, covered, overnight.

4. Shortly before serving, cut the spinach into ½-inch-wide ribbons and sauté in 2 tablespoons olive oil just until wilted. Let cool. Stir the spinach, 3 cups of water, black pepper, salt, and cayenne into the soup. Float ½ teaspoon extra-virgin olive oil on top of each serving.

Serves 6

Summer Corn and Clam Chowder

Make this hearty chowder in summer, when clams, corn, and vine-ripened tomatoes are plentiful. For a twilight supper, start with a green salad of baby lettuces and arugula. Pass thick slices of grilled Italian bread brushed with olive oil and your menu's complete.

2 tablespoons vegetable oil
6 ears yellow corn, husks and silk removed
2 tablespoons unsalted butter
1 large onion, coarsely chopped
4 garlic cloves, cut in half
Handful flat-leaf parsley stems
2 thyme sprigs or ½ teaspoon dried thyme
1 bay leaf
½ serrano or jalapeño chili, seeded and minced
1 cup white wine
2 pounds fresh littleneck clams, scrubbed
1 cup chicken broth, preferably homemade (page 75)
6 cups water
3 medium tomatoes, seeded and coarsely chopped (about 1½ pounds)

GARNISH
3 whole scallions, finely chopped

1. In a large skillet or soup pot heat the oil over medium heat and brown the ears of corn until lightly charred. Remove from the pan and set aside. Melt the butter in the same pan and sauté the onion, garlic, parsley, thyme, bay leaf, and chili until the onion is soft. Pour in the wine and clams and cover the pot. Turn the heat to medium and cook the clams until their shells pop open, about 5 minutes. Transfer the clams to a bowl, discarding any that do not open.

2. Scrape the kernels from the corn cobs. Place 1 cup of the corn and all 6 cobs in the soup pot. Pour in the chicken broth and water, cover, and simmer over low heat for 1 hour. Remove and discard the corn cobs.

3. Transfer the vegetables and herbs to a food processor fitted with the metal blade. Puree, and return the mixture to the pot. Place the pot over low heat. Remove the clams from their shells and stir into the pot. Add the tomatoes.

4. To serve, ladle into soup bowls and garnish with scallions.

Serves 8

Mediterranean Fish Stew

The special flavor of this adaptation of the classic Italian zuppa di pesce *comes from the rich variety of fish and shellfish used. Feel free to make substitutions, depending on what is fresh at your fish market, as long as the total amount remains more or less the same. Just don't use fish with a high fat content, such as tuna, mackerel, or salmon.*

¼ cup plus 2 tablespoons olive oil

1 medium onion, coarsely chopped

½ bunch fresh flat-leaf parsley

8 marjoram sprigs or 2 teaspoons dried marjoram

8 thyme sprigs or 2 teaspoons dried thyme

2 bay leaves

2 celery stalks, coarsely chopped

15 garlic cloves

Coarse salt

¼ teaspoon crushed red pepper

2 pounds fish bones, from snapper, bass, or other white-fleshed fish in the stew

1 pound ripe tomatoes, seeded and coarsely chopped, or one 15-ounce can whole tomatoes with the juices

2 tablespoons tomato paste

¼ teaspoon saffron threads (optional)

2 bay leaves

1 cup red wine

2 cups chicken broth, preferably homemade (page 75)

3 cups water

16 mussels

16 littleneck clams

16 medium shrimp, peeled

One 3- to 4-pound red snapper, striped bass, or other white-fleshed fish, filleted and cut into chunks

2 large waxy white or red potatoes, boiled until tender and cut into 1-inch cubes

16 cleaned small squid, tentacles intact, bodies cut into ½-inch rings

Coarsely ground black pepper to taste

GARNISH
Chopped fresh flat-leaf parsley

1. In a 5-quart stockpot warm ¼ cup of the olive oil over low heat. Add the onion, parsley, marjoram, thyme, bay leaves, celery, 10 cloves of the garlic, ½ teaspoon salt, and the crushed red pepper. Sauté for 10 minutes, until the onions and garlic are light golden in color. Add the fish bones, tomatoes, tomato paste, saffron if using, bay leaf, red wine, chicken broth, and water. Simmer for 30 to 40 minutes, until the fish bones are falling apart.

2. Place a colander or a strainer over a large bowl or another pot and pour the contents of the stockpot through it. Press the vegetables and fish bones as dry as you can; the last drops of the liquid are the most flavorful. Set it aside and discard the bones and vegetables.

3. Roughly chop the remaining 5 cloves of garlic. Heat the remaining 2 tablespoons of olive oil in a pan large enough to hold the rest of the ingredients comfortably. Sauté the garlic until lightly colored. Add the mussels, clams, shrimp, chunks of red snapper, and potatoes. Pour in the reserved fish broth and bring to a gentle boil. Cover and cook for 5 minutes, until the clams and mussels just start to open. Add the squid and cook for 1 or 2 minutes without shaking or stirring the pan. Season to taste with salt and pepper.

4. Spoon into bowls and garnish with parsley.

Serves 8

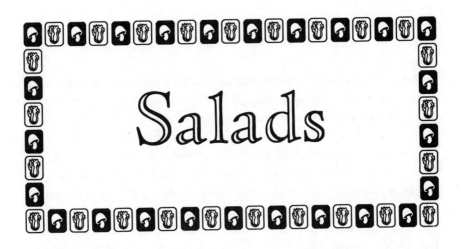

Salads

Living as we do in Southern California, with an astonishing variety of fresh produce abundant and available to us year-round, we can enjoy interesting and unusual salads every day. But the truth is, you don't need exotic ingredients to make a great salad. You can compose a great salad from ingredients you probably already have in your refrigerator or that are readily available in the supermarket. A few years ago we were invited to prepare a salade niçoise for a fancy dinner at a restaurant in Florida, and the special greens we had ordered arrived in terrible shape, completely wilted. So instead of the gourmet greens we had planned on we had to use the more standard greens—Boston lettuce, romaine, escarole, etc.—we found in the refrigerator. What we did to make the salad more interesting was to add lots of fresh herbs: basil, long-cut chives, flat-leaf parsley, and dill. No one missed the fancy lettuce.

Baby lettuce, that is lettuce that is cultivated to be much smaller and more tender than regular lettuce, is lovely in salad, but it isn't essential by any means. It's the freshness and variety of greens that are important. You can take some leaves of Boston lettuce, for example, combine them with hearts of romaine, add a little bit of radicchio (it's expensive, but a very small amount provides a nice accent) and whatever fresh herbs you happen to like, toss with a light dressing like our Basic Vinaigrette, and you'll have a wonderful green salad that could take its place on the menu with virtually any dish in this book. And don't overlook edible flowers like nasturtium blossoms that may be growing in your garden; they add visual interest and extra flavor to salad.

As a side dish or a main course for family or for company dinners, salads are versatile, nutritious, and quick. They're also just about perfect for those times when you find yourself eating alone since there's no major cooking or clean-up required. When Nancy is so busy in the restaurant or the bakery that she doesn't have time for a sit-down meal, she'll often stand in front of the open refrigerator and select chunks of meat, lettuce, hard-boiled eggs, green olives, marinated white beans, tomatoes, and shards of parmesan to eat with her fingers. She could assemble the same ingredients on a plate, but then she would have to wash more than her hands.

Garbanzo Salad with Oven-dried Tomatoes

Although Mark doesn't particularly like garbanzos (chick peas), Nancy does—hence this recipe. The flavor really improves if the salad is made the night before serving. It's wonderful with cold chicken.

1 pound dried garbanzos
2½ cups chicken broth, preferably homemade (page 75)
2½ cups water
2 large garlic cloves
2 flat-leaf parsley sprigs
2 thyme sprigs
½ teaspoon coarsely ground black pepper
½ teaspoon coarse salt

VINAIGRETTE
2 tablespoons white wine vinegar
1 teaspoon lemon juice
½ teaspoon coarsely ground black pepper
½ teaspoon coarse salt
1 garlic clove, minced
6 tablespoons extra-virgin olive oil

18 Oven-dried Tomatoes (recipe follows)
2 heads chicory or frisée

1. In a large bowl cover the garbanzos with water and allow to soak overnight.

2. The next day drain the garbanzos, rinse thoroughly, and place in a large soup pot over low heat. Stir in the broth, water, garlic, parsley, thyme, pepper, and salt. Cover the pot and simmer for 3 hours to 3 hours 30 minutes, until the garbanzos are tender but not mushy. Add more water if the liquid is absorbed before the garbanzos are done. Remove the parsley and thyme sprigs. Cool to room temperature while making the vinaigrette.

3. In a small bowl whisk together the vinegar, lemon juice, pepper, salt, garlic, and olive oil. Pour over the garbanzos and toss to combine. Cover and chill overnight. Remove the garbanzos with a slotted spoon to a serving bowl.

4. When ready to serve, cut the tomatoes into ¼-inch strips. Remove and discard the outer leaves of the chicory and chop the tender inner leaves into 1-inch pieces. Add the tomatoes and chicory to the garbanzos, gently tossing to combine. Adjust seasonings if necessary.

Serves 6 as side salad

Oven-dried Tomatoes

Dried tomatoes packed in olive oil are available in specialty shops and some supermarkets, but they are very expensive and sometimes contain unwanted preservatives and additives. Tomatoes can be dried in the oven at home rather than under the sun. Either way the dried tomatoes lend character to salads, pastas, and tomato sauces.

3 pounds plum or vine-ripened small regular tomatoes
Coarse salt
Coarsely ground black pepper
Olive oil
Capers (optional)
Fresh basil (optional)

1. Slice the tomatoes in half lengthwise and lay them, skin side down, on a baking sheet, wedging them in as tight as possible—the tomatoes will shrink greatly. Sprinkle lightly with salt and pepper and place the baking sheet on the oven rack. Turn the oven to the lowest possible setting, and leave undisturbed for 24 hours.

2. The next day, check to see if the tomatoes have shrunk to a third of their original size and most of the moisture has evaporated from the centers. If they still feel spongy, continue drying for another 10 to 12 hours, until flat and shriveled but not crisp. Remove from the oven and cool to room temperature.

3. Pack into jars and cover with olive oil. If desired, layer the tomatoes with capers and basil leaves before covering with oil. They will keep for several months in the refrigerator.

Makes 30 to 36 halves

Lentil Salad with Vegetables and Goat Cheese

Even though lentils may seem winterish, they make a lovely luncheon salad for summer. With the goat cheese omitted, the salad is very nice with grilled fish.

1 tablespoon olive oil
1 onion, finely chopped
2 large garlic cloves, finely chopped
1 bay leaf
¼ cup chopped celery leaves
1 teaspoon coarse salt
¼ teaspoon coarsely ground black pepper
1 pound dark green French lentils, washed and picked through
¾ pound smoked ham hock, skin scored on all sides
3 cups water
1 cup chicken broth, preferably homemade (page 75)

VINAIGRETTE
⅓ cup red wine vinegar
¾ cup extra-virgin olive oil
1 teaspoon coarsely ground black pepper
1 teaspoon coarse salt

1 cup diced carrots, cooked until tender
1 cup corn kernels, cooked until tender (about 1½ ears)
½ cup chopped fresh flat-leaf parsley
2 tablespoons chopped fresh thyme or 1 tablespoon dried
     thyme
4 ounces chèvre, cut into cubes
4 scallions, including some green, finely chopped
4 cups shredded lettuce

GARNISH
Cherry tomatoes, halved

1. In a large soup pot heat the olive oil over medium heat and sauté the onion and garlic until soft. Stir in the bay leaf, celery leaves, salt, and pepper. Add the lentils, ham hock, water, and broth. Cover and cook over low heat for about 1 hour, until the lentils are tender and all the liquid has been absorbed. Remove from the heat and remove the ham hock and bay leaf. Cool to room temperature, cover, and chill. This can be done a day ahead.

2. Whisk all the ingredients for the vinaigrette together in a large bowl. Pour in the chilled lentils and stir. Add the carrots, corn, parsley, and thyme. Gently stir in the chèvre and scallions.

3. Spread the shredded lettuce on plates, arrange the salad on top, and garnish with the tomatoes.

Serves 8

Note: French lentils retain their shape and firmness after cooking better than regular lentils.

Celeriac Coleslaw

Celeriac (celery root) is a knotty brown bulb with light green celery-tasting leaves. It has a mild celery flavor and the texture of a soft carrot. More common in France and Germany than here, it is used either raw or cooked, in salads and mashed with potatoes. We like to serve this slaw with grilled or roasted fish.

2 celery roots, with leaves if possible (about 1¼ pounds each)
¼ head red cabbage
Coarse salt
½ cup Homemade Mayonnaise (page 126)
1 teaspoon caraway seeds
White wine vinegar and coarsely ground black pepper to taste

1. Trim the leaves from the celery roots and reserve. Peel the skin and "knots" from the bulb. Cut each bulb in thirds through the stem end, then in half crosswise. Slice into ¼-inch julienne. Place the celery root in a colander and toss with 1 tablespoon salt. Let stand for 15 minutes to soften.

2. Finely shred the cabbage, toss with 1 teaspoon salt, and drain in a separate colander. Do not mix the two together because the cabbage will discolor the celery root.

3. Rinse both vegetables and spin dry or pat dry with paper towels. Place in a medium bowl and mix with the mayonnaise and caraway seeds. Season to taste with white wine vinegar and black pepper if necessary. Finely chop the reserved celery-root leaves and toss with the coleslaw.

Serves 6 as a side salad

Wedge of Iceberg
with Blue Cheese Dressing

Iceberg is not our favorite variety of lettuce except in this simple salad, a childhood favorite of Nancy's. Very crisp, very cold, and rather bland, iceberg is the perfect foil for the sharp and creamy blue cheese. The salad is great with steak.

1 small head iceberg lettuce, dark outer leaves removed
4 ounces blue cheese
2½ tablespoons sherry vinegar
½ teaspoon coarsely ground black pepper
1 teaspoon chopped fresh thyme or ½ teaspoon dried thyme
1 garlic clove, minced
½ cup extra-virgin olive oil

1. Cut the lettuce in half through the stem end and remove the core. Cut each piece in half. Place the wedges on chilled salad plates.

2. In a small bowl crumble half the blue cheese. Add the vinegar, pepper, thyme, and garlic. Whisk in the oil until well combined.

3. Evenly distribute the dressing over the lettuce wedges. Crumble the remaining blue cheese on top and serve immediately.

Serves 4 as a side salad

Roasted Potato Salad

Potatoes now come in many colors, including yellow and purple, but we still like the very small red ones best. Use this recipe to replace your traditional summer potato salad. Roasting gives the potatoes extra flavor, and the vinaigrette is much lighter and healthier than mayonnaise.

3 pounds tiny red potatoes
Olive oil
Coarse salt
Coarsely ground black pepper

VINAIGRETTE
1 tablespoon lemon juice
1 tablespoon Dijon mustard
2 garlic cloves, finely chopped
1 tablespoon chopped fresh thyme or 1 teaspoon dried thyme
5 tablespoons white wine vinegar
½ teaspoon coarse salt
1 teaspoon coarsely ground black pepper
1¼ cups extra-virgin olive oil

½ small white onion, thinly sliced
2 celery stalks, thinly sliced
8 scallions, including some green, finely chopped
2 tablespoons chopped fresh chives
1 tablespoon chopped fresh flat-leaf parsley

1. Preheat the oven to 400° F.

2. Wash the potatoes and lightly coat them with olive oil. Spread out on a cookie sheet and generously sprinkle with salt and pepper. Bake for 30 to 35 minutes, turning several times. Potatoes should feel tender when pierced with the point of a knife. Cut in half if larger than 1 inch and set aside to cool to room temperature.

3. Meanwhile, prepare the vinaigrette. In a medium bowl whisk together the lemon juice, mustard, garlic, thyme, vinegar, salt, and pepper. In a slow steady stream whisk in the olive oil until completely incorporated. Vinaigrette may be made 2 days ahead and refrigerated. Before using return to room temperature and shake.

4. In a large bowl toss together the potatoes and half of the vinaigrette. (Reserve the remainder for another salad.) Add the sliced onion, celery, and three-fourths of the scallions. Toss well. Set aside for 1 to 2 hours. When ready to serve, sprinkle with the remaining scallions, the chives, and parsley.

Serves 6 as a side salad

Chopped Vegetable Salad

This is a beautiful salad incorporating very common ingredients. It's also a great way to use up leftover vegetables. There is enough variety here to satisfy a grown-up appetite and yet enough familiar vegetables to make the salad appealing to children. We have given amounts to serve six generously, but we don't worry too much about proportions, and neither should you.

VINAIGRETTE
2 tablespoons commercial mayonnaise
2 teaspoons Dijon mustard
¼ cup lemon juice
2 garlic cloves, finely chopped
1 teaspoon coarse salt
2 teaspoons coarsely ground black pepper
1¼ cups olive oil

1 cup fresh corn kernels (about 1½ ears)
½ pound green beans, tips and strings removed, cut into ¼-
    inch lengths
1 kohlrabi or large turnip, peeled and cut into ¼-inch julienne
2 carrots, peeled and cut into 2 × ¼-inch julienne
½ pound asparagus, cut into 1-inch diagonal pieces (optional)
6 new potatoes, diced
4 celery stalks, cut into 2 × ¼-inch julienne
5 plum tomatoes, halved, seeded, and diced
4 ounces prosciutto, cut into strips (about 8 slices)
½ medium red onion, finely chopped
2 firm small avocados, peeled and diced
¼ cup chopped fresh chives
⅓ cup finely chopped fresh flat-leaf parsley
Torn lettuce (optional)

1. In a medium bowl whisk together the egg yolks, mustard, lemon juice, garlic, salt, and pepper. Slowly whisk in the olive oil. Set aside. (The vinaigrette may be made 2 or 3 days ahead, covered, and refrigerated. Bring to room temperature and shake before using.)

2. In a large pot of boiling salted water, blanch the corn, beans, kohlrabi or turnip, carrots, and asparagus, if using, for 3 to 4 minutes. Drain and immediately plunge into ice water.

3. In another pot boil the potatoes in salted water to cover until tender, 10 to 15 minutes. Cool to room temperature.

4. Arrange the individual vegetables in rows on a serving platter (this way, children can pick and choose the vegetables they want to eat) with strips of prosciutto in the center. Drizzle with vinaigrette and sprinkle with chives and parsley. Or toss the vegetables with a small amount of torn lettuce and the vinaigrette in a large bowl.

Serves 6

Variation: In lieu of prosciutto, cooked, crumbled bacon is always popular.

Seafood Salad

A seafood salad can be a first course, or it can be expanded into a luncheon dish. Pick whatever is fresh at your favorite fish market. Use all or some of the seafood listed, in more or less equal proportions, totaling three pounds for six servings.

6 tablespoons olive oil
5 garlic cloves, minced
1 cup white wine
Grated zest of 1 lemon
1 tablespoon plus 1 teaspoon finely chopped fresh basil
1 tablespoon plus 1 teaspoon finely chopped fresh flat-leaf
    parsley
2 shallots, minced
Crushed red pepper

SHELLFISH
Small clams in shell, scrubbed
Small mussels in shell, scrubbed and debearded
Baby octopus tentacles, cut into ½-inch pieces
Small squid, cleaned and cut into ½-inch rings
Medium shrimp, shelled
Bay scallops

VINAIGRETTE
⅓ cup extra-virgin olive oil
1 tablespoon lemon juice
¼ cup pitted kalamata olives, cut into slivers
2 tablespoons large capers, rinsed and drained
1 small head radicchio

1. In a large skillet heat 3 tablespoons of the oil, half of the garlic, ½ cup of the wine, the lemon zest, 1 tablespoon basil, 1 tablespoon parsley, and half the minced shallots.

2. Scrub outsides of clams and mussels and drop into the skillet. Immediately cover and steam until the shells open (about 5 minutes). Remove with a slotted spoon to a platter to cool.

3. Add the remaining ½ cup wine to the liquid left in the skillet and cook the octopus for 15 minutes, until tender. Then add the squid and cook 2 to 3 minutes longer.

4. Discard the liquid in the pan and add the remaining 3 tablespoons olive oil, the remaining minced garlic and shallots, a pinch of red pepper, 1 teaspoon basil, and 1 teaspoon parsley. Sauté the shrimp until they turn pink, about 2 to 3 minutes. Remove from the pan and sauté the scallops in the same oil. Cook 3 minutes. Set aside.

5. While the seafood is cooling to room temperature, stir together the ingredients for the vinaigrette. Mix together with all the seafood and mound on radicchio leaves on a platter, placing the clams and mussels, still in their shells, around the edges.

Serves 6 as a main course or 8 as an appetizer

Spinach Salad with Steak and Eggplant

Raw spinach has more flavor, color, and strength than lettuce, so it marries well with steak and browned eggplant for a fast, light dinner. If you happen to have leftover rare steak, use it, brought to room temperature.

1 pound fresh spinach
1 medium eggplant
Coarse salt
¼ cup extra-virgin olive oil
4 large garlic cloves, thinly sliced
¾ pound sirloin steak, trimmed of all fat
Coarsely ground black pepper
¼ cup chopped fresh oregano

VINAIGRETTE
2 teaspoons Dijon mustard
1 tablespoon lemon juice
1 tablespoon red wine vinegar
¼ teaspoon coarsely ground black pepper
½ cup extra-virgin olive oil

1. Wash and stem the spinach and dry in a salad spinner or between paper towels. Set aside.

2. Peel the eggplant, cut it lengthwise, and slice it into strips ⅓ × 2 × 5 inches. Sprinkle with salt and spread out on paper towels for 30 minutes.

3. Heat the olive oil in a medium skillet, add the garlic, and cook over medium heat until golden brown. Remove the garlic, reserving the oil in the skillet, and set aside. Pat the eggplant slices dry and sauté until browned on both sides. Drain on paper towels and set aside. Salt and pepper the steak and quickly sear it on both sides over high heat in the same skillet, about 6 minutes total. Cut the steak into ¼-inch slices. Set aside.

4. In a small bowl whisk together the mustard, lemon juice, vinegar, and pepper. Slowly whisk in the olive oil.

5. To assemble the salad, toss the spinach and oregano leaves with the vinaigrette and divide among 4 plates. Lay slices of eggplant around the edge, alternating and overlapping with slices of steak. Sprinkle each salad with the garlic slices.

Serves 4 as a main dish

Variation: Sauté ¼ pound oyster or large white mushrooms and toss them into the salad along with the other ingredients.

Chicken Salad with Napa Cabbage and Greek Olives

Chefs are always creating a new chicken salad. We're especially fond of this one, in which the chicken is dressed with a light, herb-flecked vinaigrette. Poaching rather than roasting the chicken assures that it will be moist and plump. And when you are finished, you have the beginnings of a good chicken stock. Because this salad relies on cabbage instead of lettuce for support, it doesn't collapse as quickly, making it a good choice for a picnic. Piled on top of crusty olive bread (or other peasant bread), this also makes terrific chicken salad sandwiches.

VINAIGRETTE
1 cup extra-virgin olive oil
3 garlic cloves, finely chopped
2 tablespoons lemon juice
2 tablespoons white wine vinegar
1 tablespoon chopped fresh thyme or 1 teaspoon dried thyme
1 tablespoon chopped fresh flat-leaf parsley
2 teaspoons chopped fresh mint
¼ teaspoon coarse salt
½ teaspoon coarsely ground black pepper

One 3½- to 4-pound whole chicken
1 celery stalk, cut into 2-inch pieces
1 carrot, cut into 2-inch pieces
4 garlic cloves
½ large onion
6 whole peppercorns
1 teaspoon coarse salt
1 medium head Napa or Chinese cabbage, shredded (about 4
    cups)
1½ cups pitted kalamata olives
½ cup chopped scallions, including some green

GARNISH
3 tablespoons chopped fresh flat-leaf parsley

1. In a small bowl whisk together all the ingredients for the vinaigrette and set aside for at least 1 hour, or refrigerate overnight.

2. In a large stockpot bring to a boil enough water to cover the chicken. Add the chicken, celery, carrot, garlic, onion, peppercorns, and salt. Lower the heat to a simmer and poach the chicken for 40 minutes. Cover the pot, turn off the heat, and leave the chicken in the broth for another 15 minutes. Remove from the broth and set aside to cool.

3. When the chicken is cool remove the skin and pull the meat off the bones. This way, rather than cutting, the chicken retains its moisture and tender texture. Place in a large bowl. Top with the cabbage, olives, and scallions. Pour on the vinaigrette and toss well with your hands. Garnish with parsley.

Serves 6 as a main course

Red Cabbage and Prosciutto Salad

Hearty red cabbage needs to be matched with ingredients of equal strength and character—in this case, prosciutto and onions. A beautifully colored salad that we like to serve with roasted meats or chops.

½ large head red cabbage or 1 whole small head
2 tablespoons coarse salt
½ small white onion, sliced paper thin

VINAIGRETTE
1½ tablespoons white wine vinegar
1½ tablespoons whole-grain mustard
¼ teaspoon coarse salt
½ teaspoon coarsely ground black pepper
½ cup extra-virgin olive oil

6 ounces prosciutto (about 12 slices)
4 scallions, green parts only, finely chopped

1. Finely shred the red cabbage, place in a colander, and sprinkle with salt. Toss well and let stand for 30 minutes. Rinse thoroughly and dry well in a salad spinner or with paper towels. Transfer the cabbage to a salad bowl and mix in the sliced onion.

2. In a small bowl whisk together the vinegar, mustard, salt, pepper, and olive oil. Pour over the cabbage and onion and toss to coat. Arrange the prosciutto slices around the edge of the bowl and sprinkle the salad with chopped scallions. Or serve on individual plates, mounding the salad in the center of the plate, wrapping the prosciutto (about 3 slices to a serving) around the cabbage, and sprinkling each salad with chopped scallions.

Serves 4 as a side salad

Fennel Salad
with Pancetta and Olives

When buying fennel, choose a bulb that is heavy for its size. This tells you that it is young and tender. Pungent Greek olives and peppery pancetta make a flavorful menage à trois *with the fennel.*

½ pound pancetta or slab smoked bacon, cut into ½-inch dice
2 fennel bulbs
1 tablespoon coarse salt
2 tablespoons white wine vinegar
5 tablespoons extra-virgin olive oil
¼ teaspoon coarsely ground black pepper
½ cup kalamata olives, pitted

1. In a skillet sauté the pancetta until browned but not crisp. Drain on paper towels and set aside.
2. Trim the feathery greens from the fennel bulbs and reserve. Cut ¼ inch off the stem end lengthwise and discard. Cut each bulb in half through the stem end, lay cut side down, and slice into ¼-inch strips. Place in a colander and toss with coarse salt. Let stand for 10 minutes to soften. Rinse and dry thoroughly in a salad spinner.
3. Place the fennel in a medium bowl and toss with the vinegar, olive oil, and pepper. Add the pancetta and olives and mix together with your hands or 2 spoons. Finely chop the reserved fennel greens and add to the salad. Serve immediately.

Serves 4 as a side salad

Composed Salad of Honey-poached Pears and Escarole

Any pear can be used here, but the Bosc, a firm, winter variety, is our choice. The pears don't have to be perfectly ripe, and if prepared a day or two in advance, they can wait in their poaching liquid to be assembled with the greens at the last minute.

This makes an elegant first course for entertaining. Try it on your menu with Boneless Pork Roast (page 220).

½ cup white wine
½ cup white wine vinegar
3 tablespoons honey
2 strips lemon zest
2 thyme sprigs
1 mint sprig
2 cups water
4 firm Bosc pears (2 pounds)
1 head escarole
2 tablespoons extra-virgin olive oil
¼ teaspoon coarse salt
¼ teaspoon coarsely ground black pepper
4 ounces blue cheese, crumbled (about ½ cup)
½ cup chopped toasted walnuts

1. In a medium saucepan combine the wine, vinegar, honey, lemon zest, thyme, mint, and water. Bring to a simmer over medium heat and cook for 10 minutes.

2. Peel the pears, leaving the stems attached. Stand the pears in the poaching liquid and cover the pan. Lower the heat and cook for 30 minutes, until the pears are tender when pierced with a knife. Remove from the heat and let cool to room temperature. Refrigerate in the poaching liquid overnight, covered.

3. When ready to assemble the salad, trim the outer leaves from a head of escarole and fan several of the nicer ones on each of 4 plates. Chop the remaining leaves and toss in a bowl with the olive oil, salt, pepper, and 3 teaspoons of the poaching liquid. Slice the pears in half lengthwise. Cut out the cores. Lay 2 halves, cut side down, on each plate. Cut ¼-inch slices along the length of each half, without cutting all the way through. Surround the pears with the chopped escarole and sprinkle with the blue cheese and walnuts.

Serves 4 as a first course

Bread Salad

Bread salad is an authentic Italian dish, panzanella. *In dialect the word means "little swamp," which, considering the ample amount of olive oil and juicy tomatoes, is quite an accurate translation! A crusty, peasant-type loaf of bread is essential here, as are the most flavorful oils. This salad is filling enough to stand alone as a luncheon dish, but it can also be served with roasted meat.*

VINAIGRETTE

1½ tablespoons walnut oil
2½ tablespoons extra-virgin olive oil
4 garlic cloves, minced
1 tablespoon lemon juice
1 tablespoon sherry vinegar or white wine vinegar
¼ teaspoon coarse salt
½ teaspoon coarsely ground black pepper

1½ tablespoons extra-virgin olive oil
1½ tablespoons walnut oil
1 garlic clove, minced
4 cups 1-inch bread cubes with crusts, cut from walnut or
    country wheat bread
6 tablespoons chopped fresh flat-leaf parsley
1 tablespoon chopped fresh mint
2 cups seeded and diced plum tomatoes
½ cup toasted walnut halves
2 to 3 cups (loosely packed) arugula leaves

1. In a small bowl whisk together all the ingredients for the vinaigrette. Let stand for 1 hour.

2. Preheat the oven to 300° F.

3. In a large skillet heat the olive and walnut oils and add the garlic. Toss in the bread cubes and stir until the bread is lightly browned. Transfer to a baking sheet and place in the oven for 20 minutes to crisp. Remove and let cool to room temperature.

4. In a large bowl combine 4 tablespoons of the parsley, the mint, tomatoes, walnuts, and arugula. Add the bread cubes and spoon on half of the vinaigrette. Toss well and add the remaining vinaigrette as needed. Sprinkle with the remaining parsley.

Serves 4 to 6

Rare Tuna
Salade Niçoise

We have always loved the classic French salade niçoise. By substituting medallions of seared tuna for the traditional tuna chunks and Tapenade for the niçoise olives, and composing the potatoes, haricots verts *(very fine green beans), and hard-boiled eggs on a bed of lettuce instead of having them together, the eye as well as the palate has something new to feast on.*

The tuna must be very fresh sashimi grade since it is not cooked through to the center. It retains its velvety texture and characteristic red color. Depending on proportions, this can be arranged on plates for a first course or on a platter for a main-dish salad.

8 to 10 ounces sashimi-grade tuna, in 1 piece
2 tablespoons olive oil
Coarse salt
Coarsely ground black pepper
16 small red potatoes, washed but not peeled
¾ pound *haricots verts,* tips removed
4 cups mixed baby lettuces or 1 large head butter lettuce,
    outer leaves removed
½ cup Basic Vinaigrette (recipe follows)
⅓ cup Tapenade (page 65)
2 hard-boiled eggs (cooked for 8 minutes)

1. Prepare a barbecue grill.

2. Brush the tuna with olive oil and sprinkle with salt and pepper. Sear on all sides over hot coals just until the very outer layer turns gray. Remove from the heat and chill while assembling the salad.

3. Preheat the oven to 400° F.

4. Toss the potatoes with 1 tablespoon olive oil and sprinkle with salt and pepper. Place in a shallow pan and roast for 30 minutes, until easily pierced with the tip of a knife. Remove from the oven and let cool to room temperature.

5. In a saucepan of boiling salted water blanch the *haricots verts* for 2 minutes. Immediately plunge them into ice water to stop the cooking.

6. To assemble the salad, toss the lettuce and *haricots verts* with ¼ cup of the vinaigrette. Arrange on individual plates or a large platter. Carefully slice the tuna into ¼-inch rounds and arrange around the edge of the plates or platter. Cut the potatoes into quarters and place between

tuna slices. Mound the Tapenade in the center of the plate and surround with quarters of hard-boiled eggs. Drizzle any remaining vinaigrette over the salad.

Serves 4 as a main course or 6 as a first course

Basic Vinaigrette

A very versatile dressing that can be substituted for other vinaigrettes in this chapter. Nothing could be more perfect on a simple green salad, except maybe adding a sprinkling of chopped fresh chives.

2 tablespoons lemon juice
2 tablespoons white wine vinegar
2 garlic cloves, finely chopped
1 tablespoon Dijon mustard
¼ teaspoon coarse salt
½ teaspoon coarsely ground black pepper
1 cup extra-virgin olive oil or ½ cup olive oil and ½ cup
    safflower oil

In a small bowl whisk together the lemon juice, vinegar, garlic, mustard, salt, and pepper. Slowly pour in the oil, continuing to whisk. Cover and refrigerate for at least 1 hour before using. Return to room temperature and shake before using. Tightly covered, this vinaigrette will keep for 1 week.

Makes 1⅓ cups

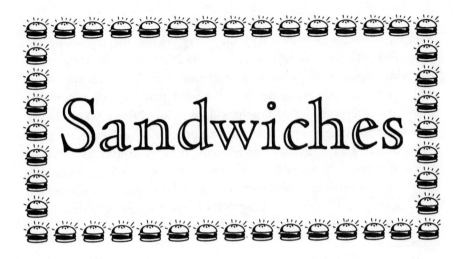

Sandwiches

Our children will eat tunafish, cheese, or egg salad sandwiches, and that's about it. Once Mark tried filling Ben's lunch box with pita bread, tabbouli salad, hummus, and stuffed grape leaves. Ben came home from school that day upset and asked for a regular sandwich from then on. He loved his lunch, it seemed, but the other kids teased him about how yucky it looked.

That doesn't mean adults can't be more imaginative. The truth is sandwiches offer endless opportunities to be creative. We hope the recipes in this chapter will start you thinking in new directions.

We feel that some of the best sandwiches are made with leftovers and other ingredients that you probably already have on hand. Look in the refrigerator and pull out leftover pork, chicken, or lamb, some peppers, cheese, sun-dried tomatoes, or eggs. Keep the shelves on the door filled with a choice of mustards—whole-grain, Dijon, tarragon—and whisk up a small batch of mayonnaise, which can be spiced for cold ingredients. Always remember that what may have been perfectly seasoned when served hot last night will lose a lot of flavor when chilled.

A sandwich can be very neat, on fine-grained white bread with the crusts trimmed, or open-faced with warm juices and mushrooms spilling over the edges. Choose your bread with your sandwich in mind. Kids often resist novelty in their lunch box, as Ben's experience shows, but at home they may be more willing to try a whole-grain or herbed bread or baguette. Toasting bread brings the flavor to the surface and adds crunch.

There's no limit to a sandwich's contents if you are ready to cook up something fresh. Mark thinks there is nothing better than an open-faced sandwich made with a delicate fillet of fish and a dollop of garlicky aïoli. Another one of our favorites—grilled eggplant and peppers with goat or ricotta cheese on focaccia bread—is served all day long at our café. Sandwiches are not just for lunch anymore. They are perfectly appropriate at any hour of the day or night.

The Perfect
Egg Salad Sandwich

The secret to great egg salad? Hand-chopping the eggs, onion, and garlic right before you plan to use them, and lots and lots of seasoning. Homemade Mayonnaise makes a difference too.

8 eggs, hard-boiled, cooled, and shelled
½ cup finely chopped red onion
3 garlic cloves, minced
1½ teaspoons coarse salt
1 teaspoon coarsely ground black pepper
1 cup Homemade Mayonnaise (recipe follows)
¼ cup fresh basil, cut into strips
2 cups watercress, stemmed
8 slices firm white bread, lightly toasted

    1. Separate the yolks from the whites of the eggs and crumble into a medium bowl. Lay the whites on a cutting board and finely chop. Add to the yolks. Stir in the onion, garlic, salt, pepper, and mayonnaise.

    2. Spread onto 4 slices of bread, sprinkle with basil, cover with watercress, and top with the remaining bread slices. Cut in half and serve.

Makes 4 sandwiches

Homemade Mayonnaise

3 eggs
2 tablespoons lemon juice
2 tablespoons white wine vinegar
1 tablespoon Dijon mustard
3 cups olive oil or 1 cup olive oil and 2 cups safflower oil
2 teaspoons white pepper
2 teaspoons coarse salt

1. In a small saucepan of boiling water, cook the eggs for 2½ minutes. Remove and immediately plunge into cold water to stop the cooking. With a sharp knife, cut each egg in half through the center. Using a small spoon, scoop out the yolks into the large bowl of an electric mixer. Discard egg whites.

2. With the mixer fitted with the whisk attachment, or in a large bowl using a hand whisk, combine the egg yolks, lemon juice, vinegar, and mustard.

3. In a slow steady stream pour in the olive oil while whisking. Continue beating until the mayonnaise is thickened. Stir in pepper and salt to taste. Cover and chill. Will keep refrigerated for 1 week.

Makes 3½ cups

Warm Mushroom Sandwich

Vary the kinds of mushrooms at will; their distinctive earthy flavors blend happily. A hearty sandwich, nearly a meal in itself, particularly welcome on a rainy day.

**12 dried shiitake mushrooms, soaked in 1 cup very hot water
for 30 minutes
1 pound white mushrooms, cut into medium slices
½ pound fresh oyster mushrooms, tough stems removed, cut
in half
10 tablespoons (1¼ sticks) unsalted butter
3 garlic cloves, cut in half
½ cup chicken broth, preferably homemade (page 75)
1 cup white wine
½ teaspoon coarse salt
4 slices walnut or crusty wheat bread, cut ½ inch thick
Olive oil
½ cup Soubise (recipe follows)**

1. Remove the mushrooms from the soaking water and squeeze out. Strain ½ cup of the liquid into a bowl and discard the rest. Remove the tough stems and chop the soaked mushrooms into ½-inch pieces.
2. In a large skillet melt 2 tablespoons of the butter. Add all the mushrooms with the garlic. Cook over high heat, covered, until mushrooms have softened and juices are released. Add the mushroom liquid, broth, wine, and salt, and continue cooking, uncovered, until the mushrooms are very soft. Add the remaining butter and stir until melted.

3. Lightly sprinkle the bread with olive oil and toast. Place a piece of bread on a plate and spread with a layer of Soubise. Spoon warm mushrooms on top of the onions and ladle any extra broth over. Serve immediately.

Makes 4 open-faced sandwiches

Soubise

This slow-cooked onion mixture is the base of the open-faced Warm Mushroom Sandwich, but it is wonderful with pork roast and chicken.

4 tablespoons (½ stick) unsalted butter
5 large yellow onions, peeled and coarsely chopped
1 cup white wine
¼ cup sherry wine vinegar
1 marjoram sprig or ¼ teaspoon dried marjoram
1 teaspoon coarse salt
½ teaspoon coarsely ground black pepper
1 tablespoon lemon juice

1. In a 12-inch skillet over moderate heat melt the butter and add the onions. Cook just until softened. Add the wine, vinegar, marjoram, and ½ teaspoon of the salt. Simmer, covered, for 1 hour 30 minutes over very low heat, stirring several times.
2. Add the remaining salt, the pepper, and lemon juice. Cook, uncovered, until most of the liquid has evaporated. Remove from the heat,

remove the marjoram sprig, and serve immediately or cool to room temperature. May be refrigerated for up to 1 week.

Makes 1½ cups

Updated Bacon, Lettuce, and Tomato Sandwich with Pepper Mayonnaise

The coffee-shop BLT is made more interesting by using a really good smoky bacon, oven-dried tomatoes instead of insipid hothouse ones, sharp-tasting peppery mayonnaise, and chewy slices of sourdough.

PEPPER MAYONNAISE

2 serrano chilies, seeded and minced
2 tablespoons minced red bell pepper
1 cup Homemade Mayonnaise (page 134)

6 thick slices smoky bacon or pancetta
6 Oven-dried Tomatoes (page 99)
2 large leaves Boston lettuce
4 slices sourdough bread, lightly toasted

1. In a small bowl stir the chilies and red pepper into the mayonnaise and set aside, covered, at room temperature for at least 30 minutes or for 2 hours in the refrigerator before using.

2. To assemble each sandwich, spread the pieces of toast generously with pepper mayonnaise. Fry the bacon until crisp and drain on paper towels. Lay 3 strips of bacon on a toast slice and top with 3 tomatoes. Lay a lettuce leaf on top and cover with the remaining toast. Cut into thirds and serve.

Makes 2 sandwiches

Open-faced Fish Sandwich with Aïoli

NANCY   *"Mark, it needs some green. Maybe some scallions sticking out. It's too white."*

MARK   *"I don't agree. It's like fish and chips, the same color."*

NANCY   *"Mark, look at it: white bread, white mayonnaise, white leeks, white fish. It needs color."*

MARK   *"What about the tomato and the parsley? I like this sandwich."*

NANCY   *"Mark, I like eighty percent—no, eighty-two percent of all you do, but this could be better. Are your feelings hurt? You said you weren't sensitive. Mark . . . ?"*

4 slices rye bread
8 tablespoons olive oil
2 large leeks
1½ pounds fillet of cod, monkfish, sturgeon, or other firm-
fleshed white fish
Flour
Coarse salt
Coarsely ground black pepper
Aïoli (recipe follows)
2 tomatoes, cored and sliced

GARNISH
Flat-leaf parsley sprigs or chopped scallions

1. Preheat the oven to 450° F.
2. Drizzle 1 tablespoon of the olive oil over each piece of bread and toast it in the oven for 5 minutes.
3. Cut a thin slice off the root ends of the leeks and discard. Slice the leeks ¼ inch thick, including 1 inch of the green. Place in a strainer and rinse thoroughly.
4. In a medium skillet heat 1 tablespoon of the olive oil and sauté the leeks over low heat until soft. Remove to a plate.
5. Cut the fish into 4 pieces. Pat lightly with flour on both sides, and sprinkle with salt and pepper. In the same skillet heat the remaining 3 tablespoons olive oil. Sauté the fish until it flakes when pierced with the tip of a knife, about 5 minutes. Remove to a plate.
6. To assemble, spread a thin layer of Aïoli on toasted bread. Cover with leeks. Top with a piece of fish, a slice of tomato, a dollop of Aïoli, and a sprig of parsley. Serve immediately.

Makes 4 open-faced sandwiches

Aïoli

This is a very rich mayonnaise made the traditional way with a marble mortar and a pestle. A heavy bowl and wooden pestle will suffice if you cannot locate a set made of marble. Take time to mash the bread and garlic together to a very fine paste. Don't chop the garlic or use a food processor or blender, which would give the garlic a bitter taste. Excellent on almost any sandwich.

1 slice white homemade-type bread, ½ inch thick
3 tablespoons white wine vinegar
6 garlic cloves, peeled and mashed
1 egg yolk
3 tablespoons hot water
1½ cups extra-virgin olive oil
3 tablespoons lemon juice
Coarse salt
Coarsely ground black pepper

1. Remove the crusts and break the bread into a small bowl. Pour in the vinegar and soak for 5 to 10 minutes. Gather the bread into a ball and press out the liquid. Place the bread in the mortar. Add the garlic and pound, pressing with a pestle for at least 5 minutes to mash the garlic and bread into a very smooth paste. Add the egg yolk and boiling water. Continue to stir until the mixture is thick and sticky. Pour in the olive oil, drop by drop, combining until thickened to the consistency of mayonnaise.

2. Switch to beating with a wire whisk to incorporate the remaining olive oil. Thin to the desired consistency with additional hot water or lemon juice. The aïoli should still be thick enough to hold its shape in a spoon. Season to taste with salt and pepper. Keeps in the refrigerator for 1 or 2 days.

Makes 1¾ cups

Three-Cheese Croustade

Nancy tasted a variation of this sandwich in France and remembers it as one of the sublime eating experiences of her life. It was served as a first course with a salad of baby lettuces dressed with lemon juice and olive oil.

Croustades are traditionally made from a long loaf of French or Italian bread cut horizontally, but we also like to use walnut or crusty wheat bread. The cheeses listed below are only suggestions; what's important is to use good melting cheeses.

Baguette or country bread, cut horizontally or into slices
Fruity olive oil
Garlic cloves, split
3 different good melting cheeses, such as fontina, aged goat
    cheese, dolce latte gorgonzola, or raclette
Fresh herbs, chopped
Cracked black pepper

1. Preheat the broiler.
2. Drizzle the slices of bread with olive oil. Run briefly under the broiler until lightly browned. Rub with garlic, top with equal amounts

of any 3 cheeses arranged separately down the length of bread, and return to the broiler just to soften. Sprinkle with chopped herbs and cracked pepper. Serve immediately.

Makes 4 sandwiches

Fresh Summer Tomato and Tapenade on Baguette

Vine-ripened tomatoes need little enhancement, but the saltiness and deep color of Tapenade make this sandwich very special. It may be necessary to cut the tomato slices in half if the tomatoes are especially large.

**1 baguette, about 2½ inches wide and 18 inches long, cut in
    half lengthwise**
4 tablespoons olive oil
½ cup Tapenade (page 65)
**1 pound very ripe tomatoes, at room temperature, cored and
    sliced ¼ inch thick**
Coarsely ground black pepper
Coarse salt

   1. Place the baguette halves, cut side up, on a baking sheet and drizzle with the olive oil. Broil until lightly browned.
   2. Spread half of the Tapenade on each half of the baguette and top with overlapping slices of tomato. Sprinkle with pepper and taste for salt. Cut each half into 3 pieces. Serve immediately.

Makes 6 open-faced sandwiches

Grilled Eggplant, Peppers, and Goat Cheese on Focaccia

This combination of flavors knows no time of day or night. We serve this sandwich all morning at our breakfast café, but it is just as much appreciated at the end of the day.

Two 6-inch rounds of focaccia
Extra-virgin olive oil
2 small Japanese eggplants, stem end removed, split
   lengthwise, and cut into 1-inch chunks
1 large red bell pepper, roasted and cut into strips
4 ounces soft goat cheese, such as montrachet
6 large basil leaves

   1. Split the focaccia in half horizontally and drizzle with olive oil.
   2. Film a pan with olive oil and sauté the eggplant chunks over moderate heat. Cook until soft and browned on all sides, about 10 minutes. Spread the eggplant on the bottom of each focaccia. Cover with strips of pepper, slices of goat cheese, and basil. Replace the top of the bread and press lightly. Cut in half and serve.

Makes 2 sandwiches

Variation: Substitute whole-milk ricotta for the goat cheese and replace the basil with frisée or chicory leaves.

Fennel, Onion, and Prosciutto on Baguette

Mark put together this sandwich the day after some friends came to dinner. The Fennel and Onion Salad had been part of an antipasto platter, and we happened to have some prosciutto left in the refrigerator. Thinly sliced hard salami would also work here, complemented by a strong whole-grain mustard.

1 baguette, cut in half lengthwise and then across
Whole-grain mustard
¼ pound arugula, stemmed
16 slices prosciutto (about ½ pound)
1 cup Fennel and Onion Salad (page 61)
Coarsely ground black pepper

    1. Lightly toast the baguette pieces and spread each with about 1 tablespoon of mustard.

    2. Cover the bread with arugula leaves and slices of prosciutto. With a slotted spoon scoop about ¼ cup of the salad for each piece and carefully lay on top of the prosciutto. Grind some black pepper over all.

Makes 4 open-faced sandwiches

Lamb and Feta Sandwich with Walnut Mayonnaise

This is a great way to use up leftover barbecued or roasted leg of lamb (pages 209 and 211).

WALNUT MAYONNAISE
¼ cup walnut oil
½ cup coarsely chopped toasted walnuts
1 cup Homemade Mayonnaise (page 126)

4 large slices sourdough bread, lightly toasted
12 to 16 thin slices roasted or barbecued lamb, trimmed of fat
1 red bell pepper, roasted and cut into strips
¼ pound feta cheese, crumbled
12 oil-cured olives, pitted
Coarsely ground black pepper

1. Add the walnut oil and walnuts to the mayonnaise and stir to combine.

2. Spread the toasted bread generously with walnut mayonnaise. Top with lamb, red pepper, feta, and olives. Sprinkle with pepper and serve.

Makes 4 open-faced sandwiches

Meatball Sandwich

In the early seventies, while Mark was in college, the ultimate Proustian taste sensation for him was a meatball sandwich. These sandwiches were probably made with canned tomato sauce and poor-quality beef, but the memory of greatness remains. Here is a recipe for an updated version of this well-loved favorite.

MEATBALLS
1 pound ground pork
1 pound ground lean beef
1 pound ground veal
1 large onion, minced (about 2 cups)
4 cups fresh bread crumbs, not dried
1 cup red wine
3 eggs
2 tablespoons tomato paste
2 garlic cloves, minced
3 teaspoons coarse salt
1 teaspoon coarsely ground black pepper
¼ cup chopped fresh flat-leaf parsley

MARINARA SAUCE
2 red onions, finely chopped
3 tablespoons olive oil
5 garlic cloves, minced
2 marjoram sprigs or ½ teaspoon dried marjoram

6 pounds ripe tomatoes, seeded and cut into ½-inch dice
4 tablespoons tomato paste
½ teaspoon crushed red pepper
2 cups red wine

Olive oil
Sautéed onions (optional)
Bell pepper strips (optional)

1. To make the meatballs, stir all the ingredients together and gently form into 1½-inch balls. Do not pack. There should be about 36. Place on a baking sheet and refrigerate, covered with plastic wrap, for at least 1 hour or overnight.

2. To prepare the sauce, in a large skillet sauté the onions in olive oil until very soft. Add the remaining ingredients and cook over moderate heat, uncovered, until the sauce is reduced by half. This will take about 30 minutes. Stir often. Remove the marjoram sprigs.

3. Remove the meatballs from the refrigerator. Coat a skillet with a small amount of olive oil and brown the meatballs over high heat. Transfer the meatballs to the tomato sauce and cook for 10 to 15 minutes. Use as a filling for a sandwich and moisten with the sauce. Sautéed onions and/or red and green peppers can be added to the sandwich.

Makes 36 meatballs, enough for 9 sandwiches

Variation: Serve the meatballs and sauce over pasta. This amount will serve 8 to 10.

Pasta

We use dried pasta at the restaurant and at home, and all of the recipes in this book have been tested with it. Because it's made with all or part semolina flour, it cooks up firmer than fresh pasta made with all-purpose flour. The quality of dried pasta has improved tremendously over the years, though imported Italian pasta is still superior in taste and texture to the domestic. There are many brands to choose from; De Cecco is one that is very reliable and widely available.

Both fresh and dried pasta now come in a rainbow of colors that result from incorporating vegetables—tomatoes, beets, spinach, red peppers, and even chilies—in the dough. Personally, we feel that these additions interfere with the texture of the pasta and provide very little extra flavor. We prefer to cook with plain pasta. To us, the sauce is what gives a pasta dish its color and distinctiveness. Plain pasta is like the surface on which you paint.

Consider the shape of the pasta when choosing a sauce to go with it. Fusilli catches the sauce better than most; rigatoni, penne (our children's favorite), or ziti can take robust flavors and chunky textures. Save the very lightest and most delicate accompaniments for capellini (angel hair) or fedelini.

Most of the pasta dishes in this chapter can be served as either a main course, with a salad or vegetable, or as a first course or side dish. Italians may be chagrined that Americans have adopted pasta as a main course, but since we Americans have broken most of the culinary rules anyway, this seems perfectly logical to us.

Fettuccine with Mascarpone and Olive Oil

This is a great light luncheon dish for a bleak wintry afternoon. We tasted something similar in Italy and loved the combination of flavors. Mascarpone is a rich Italian cream cheese that can be purchased in gourmet markets or Italian delis.

2 egg yolks, at room temperature
6 ounces mascarpone, at room temperature
¾ cup extra-virgin olive oil
1½ teaspoons coarse salt
1 teaspoon white pepper
2 garlic cloves, minced
1 pound dried fettuccine
1½ teaspoons finely chopped fresh thyme
¾ cup Freshly Toasted Bread Crumbs (recipe follows)

1. In a large mixing bowl or a food processor fitted with the metal blade beat together the egg yolks and mascarpone. Add the olive oil in a thin stream, as if making a mayonnaise. Mix in the salt, pepper, and garlic. The mixture will have the consistency of heavy cream. Transfer to a serving bowl.

2. Bring a large pot of salted water to a brisk boil and cook the pasta until al dente. Drain the pasta, add immediately to the mascarpone in the serving bowl, and toss gently to coat thoroughly. Taste and correct the seasonings, if necessary. Sprinkle with thyme and bread crumbs and serve immediately.

Serves 4 as a main course

Variation: Sprinkle with 2 ounces crumbled Roquefort or pecorino cheese.

Freshly Toasted Bread Crumbs

4 slices French or Italian bread, ½ inch thick
4 teaspoons extra-virgin olive oil
1 large garlic clove, peeled

   1. Preheat the oven to 375° F.
   2. Brush the bread slices with olive oil. Place on a baking sheet and bake just until crisp, 3 to 5 minutes. Rub each with garlic. Break up the pieces and gently crush with a rolling pin.

Makes 1 cup

Linguine with Spring Peas and Artichoke

Multicolored vegetables combine well with delicate linguine. This dish can be pulled together very quickly, making it a perfect family meal or an elegant starter for a more formal occasion. Occupy the kids with shelling peas while you prepare the artichoke.

1 large artichoke
¼ cup extra-virgin olive oil
6 tiny red potatoes, unpeeled and quartered
1 teaspoon coarse salt
1 cup fresh peas (1½ pounds in the pod)
1 red bell pepper, cut into julienne
8 scallions, finely chopped
1 pound dried linguine
1 teaspoon coarsely ground black pepper

GARNISH
1 tablespoon chopped fresh oregano

1. Cut away all the leaves of the artichoke. Cut in half lengthwise and remove the prickly choke. Slice the heart into ¼-inch wedges.

2. Pour the olive oil into a 12-inch skillet and sauté the artichoke slices and potatoes with ½ teaspoon of the salt until tender.

3. Cook the peas in a strainer in a large pot of boiling salted water for 2 minutes. Remove, reserving the cooking water, and immediately plunge into cold water. Drain and add to the skillet with the artichokes and potatoes. Add the pepper strips and scallions and lightly sauté for another 2 minutes.

4. Bring the pot of water to a boil again and cook the linguine until al dente. Drain and add to the skillet with the vegetables. Toss lightly to combine. Season with the remaining salt and the pepper and sprinkle with oregano. Serve immediately.

Serves 6 as a first course or 4 as a main course

Spaghetti with Tomato–Eggplant Sauce

This robust sauce works best with heartier pastas.

3 tablespoons plus ½ cup extra-virgin olive oil
1 teaspoon coarse salt
1 medium eggplant, unpeeled and cut into ½-inch cubes
½ large red bell pepper, finely chopped
1 medium onion, finely chopped
2 pounds plum tomatoes, cored, seeded, and chopped
¼ teaspoon plus ⅛ teaspoon crushed red pepper
4 garlic cloves, minced
1 teaspoon coarsely ground black pepper
1 pound spaghetti, ziti, penne, rigatoni, or other hearty pasta

GARNISH
½ bunch fresh basil, cut into fine shreds

1. In a medium skillet over moderately high heat, heat the 3 table-spoons olive oil with the salt. Add the eggplant and red pepper. Stir often but allow the vegetables to become slightly charred. Add the onions. Stir in the tomatoes, ¼ teaspoon crushed red pepper, garlic, the remaining ½ cup of olive oil, the black pepper, and the remaining crushed red pepper. Lower the heat, stir well to combine, and cook for 10 minutes, until thick.

2. Bring a large pot of salted water to a boil and cook the pasta until al dente. Drain and place in a large serving bowl. Pour the sauce over the pasta and toss to combine. Garnish with basil and serve immediately.

Serves 4 as a main course

Fusilli with Tomatoes and Anchovies

When heated with the tomatoes, the anchovies dissolve, leaving their elusive flavor behind for intrigue. Take care not to overdrain the pasta. A small amount of the cooking water is needed to thin the sauce and keep the pasta moist.

⅓ cup extra-virgin olive oil
½ teaspoon crushed red pepper
5 garlic cloves, peeled and thinly sliced
¼ teaspoon coarsely ground black pepper
2 anchovy fillets, drained and chopped
One 14½-ounce can whole plum tomatoes, well drained
One ¼ cup coarsely chopped pitted black olives
¾ pound dried fusilli
Juice of ½ lemon

1. In a medium skillet over high heat combine the olive oil, red pepper, garlic, and black pepper. When the garlic begins to color, add the anchovies and cook for 1 minute. Add the olives and tomatoes, breaking the tomatoes apart with a spoon. Reduce the heat to low and cook for 3 to 5 minutes. Remove from the heat and set aside.

2. In a large pot of boiling salted water cook the pasta until al dente and drain, leaving a little water on the pasta. Return the pasta to the pot, place over low heat, and pour on the sauce. Stir to combine and warm. Squeeze lemon juice over the top before serving.

Serves 4 as a first course

Fettuccine with Leeks, Walnuts, and Blue Cheese

Leeks are the mildest member of the onion family, and one that we don't use often enough. Here they blend happily with olive oil and thyme, cooking slowly to a mellow sweetness, their flavor accented with walnuts and creamy blue cheese.

4 large leeks
⅓ cup extra-virgin olive oil
½ teaspoon coarsely ground black pepper
½ teaspoon coarse salt
2 teaspoons chopped fresh thyme
1 cup chicken broth, preferably homemade (page 75)
1 tablespoon lemon juice
1 pound dried fettuccine
½ cup coarsely chopped toasted walnuts
4 ounces dolce latte gorgonzola, crumbled

1. Cut the leeks, leaving some of the green, about 8 inches long. Trim away the roots, cut lengthwise, and wash well. Dry the leeks and cut into ½-inch pieces.

2. In a medium skillet over moderate heat, heat 3 tablespoons of the olive oil and slowly sauté the leeks with the pepper, salt, and thyme. When the leeks are soft, stir in the remaining olive oil, the chicken broth, and the lemon juice.

3. Cook the pasta in a large pot of boiling salted water until al dente, drain well, and add to the leek mixture in the skillet. Remove from the heat and quickly toss together, adding the walnuts and cheese. Transfer to plates and serve.

Serves 4 as a main course or 6 as a side dish

Dutch Egg Noodles
with Mushrooms and Red Wine

*The curves and ruffles of these noodles are perfect for trapping a hearty
sauce like this. Serve as a side dish with meat or as a main dish with a salad.*

2 tablespoons unsalted butter
½ cup finely chopped onion
1 thyme sprig or ¼ teaspoon dried thyme
1 pound medium white mushrooms, thinly sliced
2 garlic cloves, minced
¼ teaspoon coarse salt
¼ teaspoon coarsely ground black pepper
5 dried shiitake mushrooms, soaked for 30 minutes in 1 cup
      hot water, cut into strips, stems discarded
2 cups red wine
¼ cup red wine vinegar
1 cup chicken broth, preferably homemade (page 75)
1 pound curly Dutch egg noodles

GARNISH
½ cup chopped fresh flat-leaf parsley

1. Melt the butter in a saucepan and sauté the onion, thyme, mushrooms, garlic, salt, and pepper over medium heat until the mushrooms are soft and all their liquid has evaporated. Add the dried mushrooms, soaking liquid (discard sediment), wine, vinegar, and chicken broth and bring to a boil over high heat. Cook for 30 minutes, until reduced by a fourth. Remove and discard the thyme sprig.

2. Meanwhile, bring a large pot of salted water to a boil, add the noodles, and cook until al dente. Drain the noodles, add to the sauce, and toss well. Sprinkle with parsley. Serve immediately.

Note: Sauce may be made 1 day ahead, refrigerated, and reheated over low heat.

Serves 4 as a main dish or 6 as a side dish

Penne Tossed with Fresh Herbs and Tapenade

The contrasting textures and flavors of this pasta dish are what is so appealing here. The freshness of the herbs lightens the intensity of the Tapenade, and the shards of parmesan add extra bite.

½ cup chopped fresh flat-leaf parsley
¼ cup chopped fresh basil
2 tablespoons chopped fresh mint
¾ pound penne
¼ cup extra-virgin olive oil
¼ teaspoon freshly ground black pepper
¾ cup Tapenade (page 65)
Juice of ½ lemon (1 tablespoon)
4 ounces parmesan, in 1 piece

1. Combine the parsley and basil in a small bowl with the mint and set aside.

2. In a large pot of boiling salted water cook the penne until al dente and drain. Pour the pasta into a medium bowl and toss with the olive oil, pepper, and lemon juice. Sprinkle with the chopped herbs and gently combine.

3. On each of 4 plates, make a circle of Tapenade around the edge, using about 3 tablespoons for each. Mound penne into the center of each circle. With a vegetable peeler or sharp knife strip off 4 or 5 shards of parmesan and arrange on top of the pasta. Serve immediately.

Serves 4 as a first course

Sautéed Penne

Parboiled and sautéed, penne can take a more robust topping than ordinary boiled pasta could.

1 pound penne or mostaccioli
4 tablespoons extra-virgin olive oil
2 cups Arrabiata Sauce (recipe follows)
4 ounces pecorino, crumbled or shaved

1. Bring a large pot of salted water to a boil and blanch the pasta for 4 minutes. Drain, toss with a little olive oil, and spread out on a cookie sheet to cool thoroughly.

2. In a large, preferably nonstick, skillet heat the olive oil until very hot. Pour in only enough pasta to spread out into a single layer. Without stirring, allow the pasta to brown on the bottom. Then stir or turn with a spatula to brown the other side. Browning the pasta will take about 10 minutes. Repeat with remaining pasta as needed to brown in a single layer. It does not have to brown evenly; if overcooked, it will become dried out.

3. Warm the sauce in a separate pan and pour half over the browned pasta. Toss until completely coated. Divide among 4 plates and spoon on additional sauce. Garnish each serving with pecorino. Serve immediately.

Serves 4 as a main course

Arrabiata Sauce

This sauce is so basic, so versatile, that there is every reason to make it in large quantities. Freeze it in pint-size containers, and you will have a pasta sauce all ready to go.

Since this is a simple tomato sauce, it is important to use the best-quality canned tomatoes. Dried chilies tend to intensify with time, so if you prefer a milder sauce, remove them once they've been sautéed with the onions. Beef broth adds richness to the sauce, but you can just use water if you prefer to keep it vegetarian.

⅓ **cup olive oil**
5 **whole dried red chilies**
2 **large onions, diced**
8 **garlic cloves, sliced**
1 **teaspoon coarsely ground black pepper**
2 **teaspoons coarse salt**
4 **cups red wine**
Two 28-ounce cans whole plum tomatoes with liquid
Two 28-ounce cans tomato puree
2 **cups beef broth or water**
Cayenne (optional)

1. In a very large sauté pan or stockpot heat the olive oil and sauté the dried chilies and onions. When the onions are soft, add the garlic, pepper, salt, red wine, tomatoes, tomato puree, and beef broth or water. Simmer, uncovered, over medium heat for 1 hour. Remove from the heat, remove and discard the chilies, and cool to room temperature.

2. Taste and correct the seasonings, adding a little cayenne if more hotness is desired. Leftover sauce freezes well.

Makes 3 quarts

Baked Fusilli and Aged Gouda

All of us grew up with our mother's own version of baked macaroni and cheese; it's a dish that's instantly associated with childhood. Vanessa and Benjamin are no exception: they'll always eat "mac and cheese." We make it with a spiral-shaped pasta. Aged Gouda cheese melts perfectly and has a rich balanced flavor.

Serve this with Oven-baked Tomato Halves (page 229) and a green salad. Or for grown-ups, as a side dish with Sautéed Spicy Catfish (page 166).

4 tablespoons (½ stick) unsalted butter
4 tablespoons flour
3 cups warm milk
1 teaspoon coarse salt
1 teaspoon coarsely ground black pepper
1 garlic clove, minced
1 pound dried fusilli
1 pound aged Gouda cheese, grated (about 3 cups)

1. In a large saucepan melt the butter and whisk in the flour until smooth. Slowly whisk in the milk and bring to a boil, stirring constantly. Continue cooking until the mixture is as thick as heavy cream, about 5 minutes. Remove from the heat and mix in the salt, pepper, and garlic. Cool to room temperature. This step can be done several hours ahead.

2. In a large pot of boiling salted water cook the pasta just until barely done. Drain. Stir 1½ cups of the cheese into the cream sauce and reserve the rest. Add the pasta and mix well.

3. Preheat the oven to 400° F. Generously butter a 9 × 13-inch glass baking dish.

4. Pour the pasta into the baking dish. Sprinkle evenly with the remaining cheese. Bake for 25 to 30 minutes, until the top is browned and crusty. The sides will look bubbly and light brown. Remove from the oven and let stand for 10 to 15 minutes before serving.

Serves 6 to 8 as a main course

Lasagna with Eggplant, Peppers, and Veal

Lasagna is time-consuming, but this updated version is so interesting and flavorful we think you'll agree it's worth the effort. Besides, it can be made in stages over several days and assembled in only fifteen minutes. We use pork and veal because they are lighter than beef.

1 medium eggplant (about 1½ pounds)
2 red bell peppers

SAUCE
2 tablespoons extra-virgin olive oil
4 medium white onions, coarsely chopped
1 pound ground pork
1 pound boneless veal, cut into 1½ ✕ ½-inch strips
⅔ cup red wine
4 garlic cloves, finely chopped
One 28-ounce can plum tomatoes, cut up, with liquid
1 teaspoon coarse salt
1 teaspoon coarsely ground black pepper
1 teaspoon dried thyme
1 teaspoon dried marjoram
½ teaspoon crushed red pepper

2 eggs
1 pound whole-milk or lowfat ricotta
¾ cup chopped fresh flat-leaf parsley
½ cup grated parmesan
1 teaspoon coarsely ground black pepper
½ pound lasagne
1 pound whole-milk or part-skim-milk mozzarella, thinly
    sliced or grated

1. Preheat the oven to 350° F.
2. Slice the eggplant lengthwise ¼ inch thick. Place on a baking sheet and bake for 30 to 40 minutes, until lightly browned and softened. Set aside.

3. Char the peppers over a gas flame or under a broiler until the skins are completely blackened. Place in a paper bag for 10 minutes to steam. Peel off the outer black skin, cut off the stem end, scrape out the seeds, and cut into 1-inch strips. Set aside.

4. Add the olive oil to a large skillet and brown the onions over high heat. Remove and set aside. Add the pork to the same skillet and brown over high heat. Remove with a slotted spoon and set aside. Add the veal strips to the skillet and brown. (Don't spread strips out over the entire pan.)

5. Without removing the veal, add ½ cup of the wine to deglaze the pan. Add the garlic, the tomatoes with their liquid, and the reserved onions and cooked pork. Stir in the salt, pepper, thyme, marjoram, and red pepper. Turn the heat to low and simmer, uncovered, for 1 hour. This sauce can be made 1 to 2 days ahead, cooled, and refrigerated. Warm through before assembling the dish.

6. In a medium bowl whisk the eggs and stir in the ricotta, parsley, parmesan, and pepper. Set aside.

7. In a large pot of boiling salted water, cook the lasagne noodles just until tender. Gently drain and separate on a large plate.

8. Preheat the oven to 350° F. Lightly oil a 9 × 13-inch pan.

9. Place 3 noodles, slightly overlapping, on the bottom of the pan. Spread a third of the meat mixture over the surface. Arrange all the eggplant slices to cover the meat. Spread with half of the ricotta mixture. Repeat the noodle and meat mixture layers. Spread the pepper strips on top, then the remaining ricotta and half of the mozzarella. Top with the remaining noodles, remaining meat, and remaining mozzarella. Place the pan on a baking sheet and bake for 40 minutes. Let stand for 20 minutes before serving.

Serves 6 as a main course

Linguine and Fresh Clams

Small Manila or Pacific butter clams are best because of their tenderness and size; just use the smallest clams you can find. If you start a pot of water boiling when you begin cooking the clams, this whole meal can be prepared in twenty minutes.

½ cup finely diced pancetta or bacon
3 shallots, finely chopped
¼ teaspoon crushed red pepper
¼ teaspoon coarsely ground black pepper
4 garlic cloves, minced
28 small clams, scrubbed, tightly closed—discard any that are
    open
1 cup white wine
¼ cup chopped fresh flat-leaf parsley
3 tablespoons chopped fresh basil
1 tablespoon chopped fresh mint
2 teaspoons grated lemon zest
1 pound dried linguine, cooked al dente and drained

GARNISH
Fresh basil

1. In a large skillet sauté the pancetta or bacon until chewy. Add the shallots, red pepper, black pepper, and garlic and cook over medium heat until the shallots are soft. Add the clams and pour in the wine. Immediately cover the skillet with a tight-fitting lid. Steam for 5 minutes. Clams are done when their shells open. Sprinkle the clams with herbs and lemon zest and remove with a slotted spoon. Add the cooked linguine to the skillet and toss with the remaining juices.

2. Arrange 7 clams around the edge of each of 4 deep plates or chowder bowls. Divide the pasta evenly and pour over any liquid left in the pan. Garnish each with a whole basil leaf.

Serves 4 as a main course

Fish and Shellfish

Our children refuse to eat any fish except canned tuna and what they have dubbed "flat fish," meaning fish like flounder, sole, and halibut that is white, mild in flavor, and, well, *flat*. They are suspicious of fish that is either colored (salmon) or thick (a tuna steak), which they find indisputable proof that the fish's flavor will be stronger than they like.

You, too, may be limited by your children's taste in fish, but it does make a wonderful grown-up dinner after they're in bed. Fish is adaptable to many quick cooking methods—sautéing, broiling, poaching, stir-frying, steaming, and grilling—and it is low in fat and calories. Economical, too, when you consider that there is so little waste. Nothing could be faster to prepare than Seared Salmon with or without its two accompanying sauces; just a few minutes over high heat is all the cooking involved. With a green salad or vegetable and rice or some other fast-cooking grain, dinner's ready. A whole roasted fish for two (page 171), with an herbed bread crumb topping, can be on the table in less than twenty minutes. And fish cooked on the bone is incredibly moist and flavorful.

Start with the freshest fish you can find, and never overcook it—these are the secrets of success with fish. Usually the freshest fish in town is in Chinatown or at an Asian food market because there is more turnover. Asians eat a great deal of fish, and the merchants are obliged to offer a good variety. You are also more likely to find whole fish, maybe even still swimming in an in-market tank.

Fish should never have a fishy smell. It should smell sweet, with a faint seawater aroma. Beware, too, of fish that has no scent at all; sometimes chemicals are used to wash off older fish, leaving it odorless. When buying whole fish, check the eyes and make sure that they are clear, not sunken or cloudy.

If you cannot find a really good fish market in your town, you may be better off using frozen fish. Many supermarkets these days have a fish counter, but the quality varies tremendously. Sometimes fish that is called "fresh" is actually as much as two weeks old. The store may have just received the fish that morning, but you don't know how long it took to get to them. Fish that is flash frozen right on the boat can, when properly thawed, have a better taste than so-called fresh fish.

Trout Fillets in Brown Butter

Trout is one of the most available fishes, and it is of consistently good quality because it is farmed. Even so-called wild trout have often been started on farms before being placed in lakes for private fishermen.

Once the preparation is completed, this dish takes only five minutes to cook and serve.

4 whole trout (¾ pound each) or 8 trout fillets
Coarse salt
Coarsely ground black pepper
All-purpose flour for dusting
5 tablespoons unsalted butter
2 tablespoons light vegetable oil
8 tablespoons red wine vinegar
6 medium shallots, finely chopped

GARNISH
Chopped scallion greens
Capers

1. Fillet the fish if using whole trout. Lightly sprinkle both sides of the fish with salt and pepper and dust with flour.

2. In a large skillet melt 1 tablespoon of the butter with the oil. Place the trout in the pan and cook over high heat until barely browned, about 3 minutes. Turn and cook for 1 minute. Remove from the pan and arrange the fillets, flesh side up, on dinner plates.

3. In same skillet melt the remaining 4 tablespoons of butter over high heat until nutmeg brown in color. Watch carefully that the butter doesn't burn. Pour in the vinegar, shallots, and a dash of salt and pepper. Stir quickly and pour over the center of each trout. Sprinkle with chopped scallion greens and capers and serve.

Serves 4

Fillet of Sole with Lemon Butter Sauce

This is about as mild and melt-in-your-mouth as fish gets. Our kids will actually eat it on occasion. Here, though, proportions are just for two because with a good bottle of white wine and a salad, this can be a very grown-up dinner for after the children's bedtime.

We like the sharpness and crunch of lightly sautéed radicchio as a side dish. You cut a small head of radicchio into quarters and quickly sear them on both sides in olive oil. Finish cooking in a hot oven for five minutes.

2 fillets of sole or other firm white-fleshed fish or salmon, skin
   removed (6 ounces each)
Coarse salt
Coarsely ground white pepper
1 tablespoon unsalted butter
1 teaspoon vegetable oil

LEMON BUTTER SAUCE
½ cup white wine
2 tablespoons chicken broth, preferably homemade (page 75)
1 tablespoon lemon juice
6 tablespoons (¾ stick) unsalted butter
1 teaspoon Dijon or whole-grain mustard
Coarse salt
Coarsely ground white pepper

GARNISH
Grated zest of ½ lemon

1. Sprinkle the fish with salt and white pepper. In a medium skillet
over medium-high heat melt the butter with the oil until sizzling. Place
the fish in the pan. Sauté for about 2 to 3 minutes on one side, or until
the edges begin to look opaque and lightly brown. Carefully turn the
fish over and sauté for another minute. Fish is done when it is firm to
the touch and flakes apart easily. Remove the fillets to a warm platter
and make the sauce.

2. Add the wine and chicken broth to the hot skillet and whisk,
loosening any browned bits from the bottom of the pan. Reduce the
liquid by half. Add the lemon juice, butter, and mustard, whisking until
the butter is melted. Season to taste with salt and white pepper. Strain
the sauce through a fine strainer.

3. To serve, place each fillet on a dinner plate and pour the sauce over. Sprinkle with lemon zest.

Serves 2

Variations: Chopped fresh herbs, such as tarragon, basil, or chervil, may be added to the strained sauce just before serving.

Green peppercorn mustard may be substituted for Dijon or whole-grain, but to retain its texture it should be stirred into the strained sauce before it is poured over the fish.

Sautéed Spicy Catfish

Long dismissed as a junk-eating scavenger on river and lake bottoms, the catfish has enjoyed renewed popularity in recent years. Most catfish found in today's markets is farm-raised and fed a high-protein diet of soybeans, corn, wheat, and vitamins. It does not taste fishy and, ounce-for-ounce, has fewer calories than a chicken breast. Catfish is a good replacement for the endangered redfish; it can take blackening without losing its natural sweetness and texture.

2 tablespoons ground coriander
2 tablespoons ground cumin
2 teaspoons coarsely ground white pepper
1½ teaspoons cayenne
½ teaspoon coarse salt
4 catfish fillets, skin removed, at room temperature (6 to 8
  ounces each)
6 tablespoons Clarified Butter (recipe follows)
2 tablespoons vegetable oil

1. In a small bowl stir together the coriander, cumin, pepper, cayenne, and salt. Spread on a large piece of wax paper. Place the fish on the seasonings and press lightly. Spoon half of the butter over the skin side of the fillets.

2. In a large skillet over high heat, heat the remaining butter and the oil. Place the fish in the pan, seasoned side down, and cook about 5 minutes, until golden brown. Carefully turn over and continue cooking another 3 minutes, until the fish feels firm to the touch when the thickest part is pressed with a finger. Serve immediately.

Serves 4

Clarified Butter

There is no substitute for the taste of butter when sautéing delicate foods like fish. Plain melted butter will burn over high heat because of its milky residue, but butter from which that residue has been removed (clarified) won't. Because much of the solids are removed, the total volume of clarified butter is about three quarters the original amount.

To make clarified butter, melt about twice the amount the recipe calls for in a roomy saucepan. Bring the butter to a slow boil and watch for several minutes until the crackling and bubbling have ceased. Remove from the heat and, without disturbing the solids that have settled to the bottom of the pan, carefully pour the clear liquid through a fine strainer into a jar. Discard what remains in the pan. Clarified butter will keep for months in the refrigerator or freezer.

Halibut with Scallion Sauce

Although the texture of halibut is wonderful, the flavor may be considered bland, making it an ideal fish for children. When Vanessa's friends come over for dinner, halibut is the flat fish they request most often. For grown-ups, the highly flavored, light green sauce we offer here adds spark and character. This dish is delicious with Horseradish Potatoes (page 245).

4 halibut fillets (about 6 ounces each)
Coarse salt
Coarsely ground white pepper
2 tablespoons olive oil

SCALLION SAUCE

½ cup white wine
½ cup Fish Stock (recipe follows)
4 tablespoons (½ stick) unsalted butter
4 scallions, cut on the diagonal into ⅓-inch pieces
6 chives, cut into 2-inch pieces
2 tablespoons chopped fresh flat-leaf parsley
1 tablespoon finely chopped shallots

1. Pat the fillets dry and sprinkle with salt and pepper on both sides. In a large skillet heat the olive oil and sauté the fish over high heat until lightly browned and easily flaked when pierced with the tip of a knife, about 6 minutes total. Remove fish to a platter and keep warm.

2. To make the sauce, add the wine to the skillet, increase the heat to high for 1 minute, and add the stock. Bring to a boil, whisk in the butter, and reduce the heat. Add the scallions, chives, parsley, and shallots and cook for 1 minute, just until scallions begin to soften. Pour the sauce over the fish and serve.

Serves 4

Fish Stock

This is the easiest stock of all to make, and it can be ready in only forty-five minutes. Make a larger amount than you need and freeze the rest. Use only the bones of white-fleshed fish.

2 tablespoons olive oil
1 celery stalk with leaves, cut into 2-inch pieces
6 garlic cloves, lightly crushed
½ large onion, thinly sliced
1 leek, including 1 inch of green, finely chopped
½ carrot, cut into julienne
6 flat-leaf parsley sprigs
3 thyme sprigs or 1 teaspoon dried thyme
½ teaspoon coarse salt
6 whole black peppercorns
1 bay leaf
1 pound fish bones, including heads, from white-fleshed fish
    like bass, halibut, snapper, or sole
2 cups white wine
4 cups water

1. Heat the olive oil in a large pot over medium heat and add all the vegetables, herbs, and seasonings. Allow to sweat and soften. Stir often and cook for 10 to 15 minutes.

2. Add the fish bones, wine, and water and bring to a low boil. Let simmer for 30 minutes. Strain through a fine-mesh strainer.

3. Let cool to room temperature, then refrigerate or freeze until ready to use.

Makes 6 cups

Roasted Whole Fish

This is a fast and light meal for two, paired perhaps with Fennel and Onion Salad (page 61). Striped bass or red snapper would be our choice.

1½ pounds whole striped bass, red snapper, or other white-fleshed fish, cleaned and scaled
2 tablespoons olive oil
Coarse salt
Coarsely ground black pepper
¼ medium onion
2 flat-leaf parsley sprigs
⅔ cup fresh bread crumbs
2 tablespoons finely chopped fresh flat-leaf parsley
1 tablespoon finely chopped fresh basil
1 tablespoon finely chopped fresh mint
1 garlic clove, minced
Lime wedges

1. Cut off the fins of the fish and trim the tail a little since it will burn in the oven. Cut 3 **X**'s about ¼ inch deep and 2½ inches long on one side of the fish. Rub the skin with 1 tablespoon of the olive oil, and salt and pepper both sides of the fish. Place the onion and parsley sprigs inside the cavity.

2. Coat an ovenproof skillet with the remaining 1 tablespoon of olive oil and place over high heat. Place the fish in the pan, slit side down, and sear, turning over to brown the other side after 2 to 3 minutes. Remove from the heat.

3. Preheat the oven to 450° F.

4. In a small bowl mix together the bread crumbs, herbs, olive oil, and garlic. Cover the top of the fish with this mixture and place in the oven. Bake until the flesh appears white through the cut nearest to the head. Time will depend on the size and thickness of the fish, but should be no more than 15 minutes. The bread crumbs will cover any imperfections and make the fish look especially appetizing.

Serves 2 or 3

Grilled Swordfish on Rosemary Branches

Swordfish is the steak of fish—meaty, flavorful, and very well suited to grilling, especially when threaded on fragrant branches of rosemary. Even when stripped of their greenery, they infuse the fish with a light perfume.

4 rosemary branches, about 10–12 inches long, stripped of all
 leaves except for 1½ inches at top, opposite end
 sharpened to a point
1½ pounds swordfish, cut into about 16 pieces, ¾ × 1½
 inches
12 bay leaves, soaked in water for 30 minutes if dried
3 tablespoons olive oil
1 tablespoon finely chopped fresh tarragon or 1 teaspoon dried
 tarragon
1 tablespoon finely chopped fresh flat-leaf parsley
¼ teaspoon coarse salt

1. Prepare a barbecue grill.

2. Alternate swordfish with 3 bay leaves on each of the rosemary
skewers.

3. Stir together the olive oil, tarragon, parsley, and salt. Coat all sides
of the fish with the mixture. (This step may be done several hours
ahead. Refrigerate, covered, and bring to room temperature again before
grilling.)

4. Grill for about 2 minutes per side, or until the fish is still slightly
pink inside. It will continue to cook after being removed from the fire.
Remove from the skewers and arrange on plates with the bay leaves.

Serves 4

Seared Scallops
with Tomato Vinaigrette

This is a wonderful, colorful summer supper we enjoy when scallops and tomatoes are in season. The best scallops are large, firm, and translucent, with a sweet aroma. Since many are packed in water and shipped, make sure to drain scallops in a colander for at least thirty minutes before cooking.

Scallops are rich and hearty, so the sharpness of the tomatoes here is a good contrast. If large enough not to fall through the grate, they are very good grilled, especially over mesquite.

1 pint cherry tomatoes (1 pound)
⅓ cup finely chopped red onion
⅓ cup niçoise olives, pitted and finely chopped
2 tablespoons minced fresh oregano or 1 tablespoon dried
    oregano
2 tablespoons lemon juice
1 teaspoon coarsely ground black pepper
¼ cup extra-virgin olive oil
1 pound fresh sea scallops
1 tablespoon olive oil
½ teaspoon coarse salt
Coarsely ground black pepper to taste

GARNISH
Chopped fresh oregano

1. Remove the stems from the tomatoes, cut in half horizontally, squeeze out the seeds, and coarsely chop. Toss in a medium bowl with the onion, olives, oregano, lemon juice, pepper, and extra-virgin olive oil. Set aside at room temperature for up to 3 hours.

2. Trim any tough ligaments from the sides of the scallops. Place in a small bowl and toss well with the 1 tablespoon olive oil, salt, and pepper. Place a heavy-bottomed pan, preferably cast iron, over high heat. When the pan is very hot and beginning to smoke, place the scallops in a single layer and lightly brown on one side, less than 1 minute. Carefully turn and brown on the other side. Do not overcook.

3. Scoop the tomato vinaigrette from the bowl and mound in the center of a platter. Surround with the seared scallops. Garnish with fresh oregano. Serve immediately.

Serves 4

Seared Salmon with Two Cucumber Sauces

For this recipe select small Japanese cucumbers if possible; they are thin-skinned and have smaller seeds and a more intense cucumber flavor. Make sure the cucumbers are not waxed, since the peel is used in the green sauce.

Although beautiful and complementary to the salmon, the two sauces can be omitted, leaving you with the simplest preparation of all. A good nonstick pan will color and sear the fish to perfection without fat.

CUCUMBER SAUCE

4 Japanese cucumbers or 1 burpless cucumber
1 tablespoon coarse salt
3 shallots, finely chopped
3 tablespoons rice wine vinegar
½ teaspoon coarsely ground black pepper
¼ cup chopped fresh dill
4 tablespoons olive oil

GREEN SAUCE

3 shallots
2 tablespoons lemon juice
4 mint sprigs
4 parsley sprigs
1 Japanese cucumber or ½ burpless cucumber
2 cups sour cream
1 teaspoon lemon juice
¾ teaspoon coarse salt
½ teaspoon coarsely ground white pepper

4 thin salmon fillets, skin on, at room temperature (6 to 8
    ounces each)
1 teaspoon olive oil (optional)
Coarse salt
Coarsely ground black pepper

1. For the cucumber sauce, peel the cucumbers, reserving the peels, and cut in half lengthwise. Scrape out the seeds and discard. Slice ½ inch thick. Place in a colander, toss with salt, and set aside for at least 30 minutes to wilt. Wash the cucumbers under running water to remove the salt and place in a medium bowl. Add the shallots, vinegar, pepper, dill, and olive oil. Set aside.

2. For the green sauce, place the shallots, lemon juice, mint, parsley, cucumber, and reserved peels in a blender or a food processor fitted with the metal blade. Blend or process until completely liquefied. Strain the sauce through a fine sieve. There should be about ½ cup liquid. In a small bowl stir together ⅓ cup of the green liquid with the sour cream, lemon juice, salt, and white pepper. Refrigerate.

3. Rub the salmon fillets with olive oil, if using, and sprinkle with salt and pepper. Heat a 12-inch nonstick skillet over high heat for 2 minutes. Lay the fillets, skin side up, in the skillet. Cook 3 to 4 minutes, turning and cooking for 2 minutes on the opposite side. The fish should just barely flake when pierced with the tip of a knife. Carefully lift the fish out of the pan. The flesh should be brown and crusty.

4. Arrange each fillet, skin side down, in the center of a dinner plate. Spoon some of each sauce on either side and serve.

Serves 4

Risotto with Mussels and Fresh Herbs

Despite the long list of ingredients, this dish comes together very quickly. Fresh herbs are essential here; dried substitutes just won't work. Mussels and saffron are a natural combination so try to add some saffron to the risotto if you can.

1 cup white wine
40 mussels, scrubbed and debearded
3 tablespoons olive oil
½ onion, coarsely chopped
4 garlic cloves, finely chopped
½ teaspoon coarse salt
¼ teaspoon coarsely ground black pepper
¼ cup chopped fresh thyme
1 pound Arborio rice
3 cups chicken broth, preferably homemade (page 75)
3½ cups water
20 to 30 saffron threads (optional)
½ cup grated parmesan
¼ cup finely chopped fresh flat-leaf parsley
¼ cup finely chopped fresh oregano
¼ cup finely chopped fresh basil
2 tablespoons finely chopped fresh mint

1. In a large saucepan bring the wine to a boil over medium heat. Add the mussels, cover, and steam for 3 to 4 minutes, until the mussels open. Discard any unopened mussels. Remove the mussels from the pan and set aside, covered, to keep warm.

2. In a large, deep saucepan or soup pot heat the olive oil and sauté the onion and garlic over medium heat until the onion is soft. Add the salt, pepper, and thyme. Stir in the rice. Set aside.

3. Pour the chicken broth and water into the pan with the wine. Bring to a simmer. Add the saffron, if using, bring to a boil, and reduce the heat to a simmer. Slowly pour this liquid into the rice mixture, ½ cup at a time, stirring constantly over medium-low heat, for about 20 to 25 minutes, until the rice is very creamy. Stir in the parmesan and fresh herbs and serve immediately, topped with mussels.

Serves 8

Shrimp in Pasilla Chili Sauce

This recipe calls for a dried pasilla chili, which can be found in Hispanic markets. Soaking the chili reconstitutes it and yields an intensely flavored liquid that enhances the sauce. This spicy shrimp dish is excellent served with a simple green salad and Rice with Toasted Flax Seed (recipe follows).

1 dried pasilla chili, split and seeded
1 cup boiling water
½ teaspoon whole coriander seeds
1 teaspoon whole black peppercorns
1½ teaspoons coarse salt
2 large garlic cloves
1½ pounds large shrimp (about 24 to 30), peeled and deveined
4 tablespoons olive oil
½ medium onion, finely chopped
6 Italian plum tomatoes, cored, seeded, and diced
¼ teaspoon ground coriander
½ cup red wine
¼ teaspoon coarsely ground black pepper
½ cup finely chopped flat-leaf parsley
Juice of ½ lime
4 lime wedges

   1. Place the chili in a small bowl, pour boiling water over it, and allow to stand for 30 minutes.

   2. Meanwhile, using a mortar and pestle or mini-chopper, chop or grind the coriander seeds, peppercorns, salt, and garlic to form a paste. Place the shrimp in a bowl and toss with the paste until well coated. Let stand 1 hour.

   3. When the chili has softened, drain the soaking liquid and reserve. Puree the chili in a blender or food processor and set aside.

4. Heat 2 tablespoons of the oil in a large sauté pan over high heat. Add the shrimp and cook just until they turn pink, about 3 minutes. Remove to a plate. Add the onion and remaining 2 tablespoons of oil and cook until the onion is translucent. Stir in the chili puree, tomatoes, coriander, wine, pepper, reserved soaking liquid, and parsley and cook over high heat for 15 to 20 minutes, until the liquid thickens.

5. Return the shrimp to the pan and stir to combine with the sauce. Squeeze the juice of ½ lime over the shrimp just before serving. Garnish each plate with a lime wedge.

Serves 4

Rice with Toasted Flax Seed

Flax seeds can be purchased in health food markets. Nancy put the seeds in the multi-grain bread we bake at La Brea Bakery, so it was natural for us to try adding them to other dishes. You will love the toasty flavor.

½ cup flax seeds
2 tablespoons olive oil
1½ cups long-grain rice
1 teaspoon coarse salt
½ teaspoon coarsely ground black pepper
1½ cups chicken broth, preferably homemade (page 75)
1½ cups water

1. Toast the flax seeds by shaking them in a small skillet over moderate heat for 8 to 10 minutes. The seeds will begin to give off a toasted aroma and change color slightly when ready.

2. Heat the olive oil in a medium saucepan and lightly sauté the rice until it whitens. Add the salt, pepper, broth, and water, bring to a boil, cover, and lower the heat to a simmer. Cook for 25 minutes or until all the liquid has been absorbed and the rice is tender. Stir in the flax seed. Fluff with a fork and serve.

Serves 6

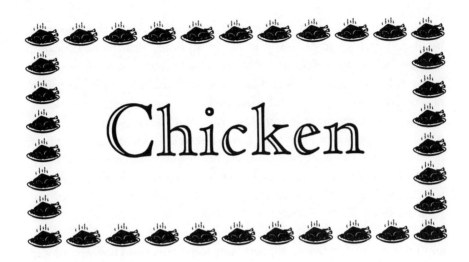

Chicken

Chicken was once a luxury food; if you could afford to have it once a week on Sunday you were living well. Now it is one of the most inexpensive sources of protein, even at the premium price asked for organically raised, free-range birds. The best chickens are locally raised. They are fresher and firmer, with a better flavor than chickens shipped long distances on ice. Wherever you live, it's worth searching out sources for local good-quality chickens.

Chicken is incredibly versatile. It can be poached, grilled, roasted, broiled, baked, or fried, and can be complemented by an amazing variety of sauces. The flavor of chicken pleases without being bullyingly assertive, and children love it. For a fast dinner on a weeknight, nothing beats chicken. Tuscan Chicken, a fryer split and stuffed under the skin with herbs and garlic, can be ready to eat in an hour. Paillard of Chicken, chicken cutlets in a delicate white wine sauce, is also very quick to prepare. Risotto with Chicken Livers takes a little more effort, but is so hearty that only a green salad is needed to accompany it.

And don't forget that if you make your own chicken broth at home, which we hope you will, you can have cooked chicken at hand for many different kinds of spontaneous meals. For a quick lunch we often toss together tender pieces of poached chicken with shredded cabbage, Mediterranean olives, scallions, and an olive oil vinaigrette and mound the salad on thick slices of olive bread.

We think you will find yourself using the recipes in this chapter over and over again, for family dinners and for company. They are simple and basic and can be varied to suit your own tastes. We hope you will be challenged to try your own adaptations. That's the great thing about chicken—choose a different seasoning, vary a sauce slightly, or change the cooking method, and you have an entirely new dish.

Southern Fried Chicken

Fry this chicken in the cool of the morning after it has soaked overnight in buttermilk. Make sure to cook plenty because you'll want to put some in your kids' lunch boxes.

Two 3½- to 4-pound chickens, cut up
4 cups buttermilk
1½ cups flour
1½ teaspoons baking powder
3 teaspoons coarse salt
½ teaspoon cayenne
2 teaspoons coarsely ground black pepper
1½ cups peanut or vegetable oil

1. Several hours, and up to 1 day, before serving place the chicken pieces in a shallow dish and pour over enough buttermilk to cover. Cover the dish with plastic wrap and refrigerate.

2. If necessary, let the chicken come to room temperature before cooking it. This is important; otherwise the outside will get too brown before the inside is cooked through.

3. Place the flour, baking powder, salt, cayenne, and black pepper in a paper or plastic bag and shake to combine. Drain the chicken and place a few pieces at a time in the bag and shake to coat thoroughly. Place the pieces on wax paper until all are coated.

4. In a large skillet heat the oil to 350° F. Carefully add the chicken and cover the pan. Lower the heat to medium and cook for 8 to 10 minutes. Turn the chicken over and continue to cook for 10 to 12 minutes uncovered. To test for doneness, cut into the thigh meat next to the bone, as this part takes the longest time to cook. If the juices run clear, the meat is done.

5. Remove from the pan and drain on paper towels. Serve immediately or at room temperature.

Serves 8

Tuscan Chicken

We discovered this traditional Italian method for cooking chicken during the time we spent in Tuscany with our children in 1986. Since then, we have made it very often. You cut through the breastbone and open up the bird so that all the parts touch the pan and cook evenly. A whole chicken cooked in this Italian country style has an irresistibly crisp, salty, herb-flecked skin and is ready in an hour.

One 3-pound whole chicken
3 large garlic cloves, sliced very thin
2 tablespoons finely chopped fresh thyme or 1 tablespoon
    dried thyme
½ cup olive oil
Coarse salt
Coarsely ground black pepper
Lemon wedges

1. Trim the second joint from the wings of the chicken; discard or save for broth. With the breast side up, cut the chicken through the center of the breastbone. Pull apart to open up the two sides, then turn the chicken over. With the heels of your hands, press firmly down on the backbone and on the thigh and leg joints to flatten the chicken as much as possible.

2. In a small bowl mix the garlic and thyme together. Starting at the tail, very gently separate the skin from the meat by sliding your hands under the skin. Spread the garlic-thyme mixture as evenly as possible all over the meat. Set aside, covered and refrigerated, for several hours or overnight.

3. About 45 minutes before serving, heat the olive oil in a 9- or 10-inch heavy skillet. Salt and pepper both sides of the chicken and place it skin side down in the hot oil. Place another heavy pan on top of the chicken, fitting it just inside the rim of the skillet. Weight it down with a brick or rock.

4. Cook the chicken over moderately high heat for 30 minutes. With a spatula carefully loosen the sides, which may have stuck to the pan, and gently lift the chicken to check the color of the skin. If not a deep, rich brown, continue cooking for another 5 minutes. Then, with a spatula or long tongs, lift the chicken without tearing the skin and turn it over to cook for another 8 to 10 minutes, or until the juices run clear. The meat should appear white and should spring back when touched. (There's no need to put a weight on the second side.)

5. Remove the chicken from the pan and place it on a cutting board to rest for 5 minutes. Cut along both sides of the backbone and between the body and the thigh. Transfer to a serving platter and arrange to resemble the original shape. Serve with lemon wedges.

Serves 4

Broiled Marinated Chicken

Every family has a favorite barbecued chicken recipe. Here is ours. The chicken, flavored with a zesty marinade, can be broiled or grilled over hot coals. It's delicious with Celeriac Coleslaw (page 102).

One 3-pound chicken, cut up

MARINADE
½ medium onion, finely chopped
⅓ cup minced fresh gingerroot
1 red chili, finely chopped, or ¼ teaspoon crushed red pepper
½ jalapeño, seeded and finely chopped
1 teaspoon coarsely ground black pepper
¼ cup lime juice
¼ cup soy sauce
¼ cup olive oil

1. If the thigh and leg of the chicken are joined, remove the thigh bone, cutting through the joint but leaving the meat attached to the drumstick. This will allow the thickest meat to cook at the same rate as the other pieces.

2. In a small glass or plastic bowl stir together the onion, ginger, chili, jalapeño, pepper, lime juice, soy sauce, and olive oil. Pour a fourth of this marinade into a nonreactive dish large enough to hold the chicken. Arrange the chicken pieces in the dish in a single layer and pour another fourth of the marinade over all. Reserve the remaining marinade for basting. Cover the dish and refrigerate for several hours or overnight.

3. With some of the marinade still clinging to the chicken, grill it over hot coals or broil it 3 to 4 inches from the heat, basting with reserved marinade. Turn the pieces after 10 to 12 minutes and continue to cook for another 10 to 12 minutes.

Serves 4

Whole Roasted Chicken

Whole roasted chicken is a little more difficult to serve than roasted chicken already cut up into serving-size pieces, but the flavor is vastly superior. In this recipe a heady herb and garlic mixture is spread under the skin, to flavor the meat more directly, and then the chicken is roasted. We have found that roasting chicken at a high temperature results in moister meat and crisper skin. Serve this with our French Fries (page 246) and the onion slices left in the pan after roasting.

One 3½-pound whole chicken, at room temperature
3 garlic cloves, minced
1 tablespoon chopped fresh rosemary or 2 tablespoons dried
rosemary
Olive oil
Coarse salt
Coarsely ground black pepper
1 onion, cut in half
½ lemon

1. Preheat the oven to 450° F.
2. In a small bowl mix together the garlic, rosemary, 1 tablespoon olive oil, ½ teaspoon salt, and ¼ teaspoon pepper. Sprinkle the cavity of the chicken with a little more salt and pepper, and place half of the onion and the lemon in the cavity. With the chicken on its back with its legs facing you, carefully loosen the skin with your fingers, moving across the breast and over the legs. Spread the herb mixture as evenly as possible over all the meat under the skin. Truss the chicken.

3. Slice the remaining piece of onion ½ inch thick and place the slices on the bottom of a lightly oiled ovenproof pan or cast-iron skillet. Lightly coat the outside of the chicken with olive oil, sprinkle with a little more salt and pepper, and place it on its side on top of the onion slices. Roast for 20 minutes. Turn the chicken to the other side and roast for another 20 minutes. Lower the heat to 350° F., turn the chicken on its back, and roast for another 10 or 15 minutes, or until the juices run clear when pierced with the tip of a knife under the leg. Remove from the oven and allow to rest 10 minutes before carving.

Serves 4

Paillard of Chicken

Chicken breast prepared in this way will be enjoyed by all. A simple bowl of spaghettini or angel hair pasta, tossed with garlic, olive oil, and grated parmesan, and Sautéed Zucchini Halves (page 228) complete the menu for the family long on hunger and short on time.

4 chicken breast halves, boned and skinned
½ cup flour
½ teaspoon coarse salt
½ teaspoon coarsely ground black pepper
2 teaspoons chopped fresh thyme or 1 teaspoon dried thyme
3 tablespoons unsalted butter
1 tablespoon light vegetable oil
¾ cup white wine
2 tablespoons heavy cream
1 garlic clove, very thinly sliced
1 teaspoon Dijon mustard

1. Place each chicken breast between sheets of oiled plastic wrap and pound with a smooth mallet or meat pounder until ¼ inch thick. On a plate combine the flour, salt, pepper, and half of the thyme. Press each piece of chicken into the mixture until it is well coated. Discard the leftover flour mixture.

2. In a large skillet over medium-high heat, melt 2 tablespoons of the butter and add the oil. Sauté the chicken quickly on each side until lightly browned. Remove to a serving platter. Pour into the skillet the wine, cream, remaining thyme and butter, garlic, and mustard. Stir together over medium heat, scraping any browned bits from the bottom of the pan. If the sauce becomes too thick, add 1 tablespoon of warm water. Pour over the chicken and serve.

Serves 4

Risotto with Chicken Livers

Be patient when making risotto: to get the beautiful, creamy texture you want, you need to take plenty of time adding the liquid. Add cooked chicken livers at the end for a satisfying and earthy meal.

½ pound chicken livers
3 tablespoons olive oil
½ onion, finely chopped
3 garlic cloves, minced
1 pound Arborio rice
½ teaspoon coarse salt
½ teaspoon coarsely ground black pepper
2 cups red wine
2 cups chicken broth, preferably homemade (page 75)
3½ cups water
¾ cup grated parmesan
6 tablespoons chopped fresh flat-leaf parsley

1. In a heavy-bottomed saucepan sauté the chicken livers over high heat in 1 tablespoon of the olive oil until seared on the outside and still slightly pink inside. Remove the livers and set aside.

2. In the same pan heat the remaining 2 tablespoons of oil over medium heat and sauté the onion and garlic with the salt and pepper until the onion is soft. Stir in the rice and combine well.

3. Combine the wine, broth, and water in a saucepan and bring to a simmer. Using an 8-ounce ladle, pour the liquid a ladleful at a time into the rice, stirring constantly after each addition until it is completely absorbed. Slowly the rice will expand and become creamy. This will take about 30 minutes.

4. When all the liquid has been absorbed, cut the chicken livers into strips and gently fold into the rice. Stir in the parmesan and 4 tablespoons of the parsley. Sprinkle with the remaining parsley and serve.

Serves 8

Chinese-flavored Chicken Wings

Since Spago had little use for chicken wings on the menu, Mark would often prepare them in this much-requested way for staff lunch.

1 cup olive oil
1½ teaspoons crushed red pepper
2 tablespoons minced fresh gingerroot
5 garlic cloves, minced
½ cup soy sauce
1 tablespoon honey
2 tablespoons red wine vinegar
1 teaspoon coarsely ground black pepper
5 pounds chicken wings, wing tips removed

1. In a small skillet combine the olive oil and red pepper, heating until the pepper begins to sizzle. Pour into a small bowl, add the ginger, garlic, soy sauce, honey, vinegar, and pepper, and whisk together.

2. Arrange the chicken wings in a shallow nonreactive pan or bowl and pour the marinade over. Turn the chicken to coat all sides. Cover and marinate for 1 hour at room temperature, turning once.

3. Preheat the oven the 325° F.

4. Spread the chicken wings in a single layer on a cookie sheet and drizzle with any marinade left in the pan. Place in the oven and bake for 30 minutes. Raise the oven temperature to 400° F. and cook the chicken for another 30 minutes to glaze and caramelize it. Pour off the excess juices, turn the chicken pieces over, and return the pan to the oven for 10 minutes.

5. Remove from the oven and let stand for 10 minutes before serving.

Serves 6 to 8

Meat

Like many American families, we are trying to eat lighter these days, enjoying more fruits, vegetables, pastas, legumes, and grains and cutting back on our consumption of meat, particularly red meat. Interestingly, many young children eat this way naturally; spaghetti, macaroni and cheese, peanut butter, and grilled cheese are universally favored foods with the younger set. But we still enjoy meat several times a week. As far as Nancy is concerned, there is nothing like a fine steak, seared to perfection. And on occasion Mark still enjoys tucking into a great meatball sandwich smothered in homemade marinara sauce.

Meats are great on the grill, and they don't have to be watched as carefully as more delicate fish or vegetables do. Big cuts of meat especially—like a whole leg of lamb—are really ideal grilled. You don't heat up the kitchen, and clean-up is a breeze.

Happily for those of us who still eat meat, it is now possible to obtain very lean cuts. Fat is the carrier of flavor in meat, but even in the very leanest and least marbled cuts there is sufficient fat to please the palate. Pork is unlike beef in that its fat is mostly around the outside. Market butchers are trimming this to a minimum to reduce the calorie count.

Remember, too, that you don't need to serve big portions of meat. It's better to eat meat less often, and in smaller quantities, but have great quality. When splurging on prime rib or veal chops, for instance, buy the very finest you can, serve small portions, and enjoy every ounce. Be aware that there's a great difference in flavor between prepackaged ground beef and beef that's been freshly ground; it distinguishes a great hamburger from ordinary one. Always go for quality when buying meat, and you can't go wrong.

Japanese Flank Steak

Kazuto Matsusaka was a line cook at Michael's when Mark worked there in 1976 (he now has his own restaurant in Santa Monica). He is a wizard with a knife and has hands as fast as a Veg-o-Matic. He could easily assemble this dish in minutes. Ordinary mortals can still prepare it very quickly.

MARINADE
½ medium onion, finely chopped
⅓ cup peeled and minced fresh gingerroot
1 red chili, finely chopped, or ½ teaspoon crushed red pepper
1 teaspoon coarsely ground black pepper
¼ cup lime juice
¼ cup soy sauce
¼ cup olive oil

2½ pounds flank steak
2 tablespoons olive oil (optional)
¼ teaspoon coarse salt

1. In a small glass or plastic bowl stir together the onion, ginger, chili, black pepper, lime juice, soy sauce, and olive oil. Pour a fourth of the marinade into a nonreactive dish large enough to hold the steak. Lay the steak on top and spread another fourth of the marinade over the meat. Cover with plastic wrap and set aside for several hours or refrigerate overnight, turning the steak once. Cover the remaining marinade and refrigerate for basting.

2. Remove the steak from the marinade and sprinkle with salt. Grill over hot coals for approximately 5 minutes per side, basting with the reserved marinade, or heat 2 tablespoons of olive oil in a cast-iron skillet and sauté the meat over high heat for 5 to 6 minutes per side. The outside of steak should be well seared, but inside it should be rare.

3. Remove to a platter and allow to rest 5 minutes. Cut into ¼-inch-thick strips against the grain.

Serves 6

Beef Shanks

Beef shanks are delicious, meaty, and very inexpensive, but they may not be available at every market. They are worth asking for, though. Request one-inch-thick slices, allowing about half a pound per serving. Beef shanks contain lots of marrow, which thickens the hearty stock. Serve these beef shanks in a bowl with Polenta (recipe follows) to soak up the flavorful broth. The shanks are also excellent with Roasted Garlic Potatoes (page 244) or Mashed Potatoes with Olive Oil and Greek Olives (page 242).

2 tablespoons olive oil
2 pounds beef shanks
1 onion, finely chopped
2 celery stalks, chopped into ½-inch dice
1 large carrot, peeled and chopped
1 tablespoon chopped celery leaves
2 flat-leaf parsley sprigs
1 bay leaf
1 teaspoon fresh thyme or ½ teaspoon dried thyme
1 cup red wine
1 cup beef broth
1 cup water
1 tablespoon tomato paste

1. Heat the olive oil in a heavy pan large enough to hold the shanks in a single layer. Sear them on both sides over high heat until well browned. Remove.

2. To the pan add the onion, celery, carrots, celery leaves, parsley, bay leaf, thyme, wine, broth, water, and tomato paste. Bring to a boil, return the shanks to the pan, cover, and simmer for 1 hour. Check after 30 minutes and add more water if needed to keep the liquid to the top of the shanks.

3. Remove the shanks, skim off the fat with a ladle, and put everything remaining in the pan into a food processor fitted with the metal blade. Puree, then press the puree through a strainer and return the liquid to the pan. Add 1 cup of water if the sauce is too thick. Discard the solids in the strainer.

4. Return the shanks to the pan and cook over very low heat for 1 hour 15 minutes, or until the meat is tender and falls away from the bone. Serve in a bowl.

Serves 4

Polenta

Polenta is, quite simply, cornmeal mush. When cold, it can be sliced and fried, grilled, or run quickly under the broiler. It is perfect with Beef Shanks (preceding recipe) or chicken or meat stew, since it absorbs the juices while retaining its texture.

1 cup chicken broth, preferably homemade (page 75)
1 cup milk
1 cup regular polenta
½ teaspoon coarsely ground black pepper
¼ cup grated parmesan
Flour for dusting
⅓ cup vegetable oil

1. In a medium saucepan bring the broth and milk to a boil. Slowly stir in the cornmeal and continue stirring until the mixture is the consistency of mashed potatoes and comes away from the sides of the pan, about 25 minutes. Add the salt, pepper, and parmesan, stirring until the cheese is melted.

2. Grease a baking dish at least 8 inches square and pour in the polenta. Smooth the top with a spatula and set aside to cool. Refrigerate, covered, or leave at room temperature for several hours.

3. Cut into triangles or diamonds about 2 × 3 inches. Dust with flour.

4. In a skillet heat the oil and sauté the pieces of polenta until lightly browned and crispy on both sides. Drain on paper towels and serve.

Serves 4

Peppered Steak

Food & Wine *magazine called a couple of years ago and asked for a menu for their article "Cooking for the One You Love." There was never any question for us what that meal would be because it's Nancy's all-time favorite: a steak of superior quality, seared on both sides and very rare in the center, a mound of thick-cut French Fries (page 246), and quickly sautéed fresh spinach (page 227).*

¼ cup whole black peppercorns
2 New York strip steaks (about 12 ounces each)
½ teaspoon coarse salt
2 tablespoons vegetable oil

1. Carefully pour the peppercorns out onto a work surface, keeping them as close together as possible. Using a very heavy, flat-bottomed pan, press hard on the peppercorns to crack them.

2. Salt the steaks on both sides and lay directly on the pepper, pressing to make as much pepper as possible stick to each side. Set aside to come to room temperature.

3. Pour the oil into a medium skillet over high heat. Lay the steaks in skillet and cook approximately 4 minutes per side for rare. Remove to a serving plate.

Serves 2

Beer-braised Brisket

The only way to ruin a brisket of beef is to let it dry out. As long as there is enough liquid in the pot, it can cook all day. Instead of slicing brisket across the grain, we like to pull it apart into strings. The kids particularly enjoy this as it reminds them of eating Armenian string cheese. Brisket is certainly a perfect weekend family meal and one that provides great weekday leftovers too. Serve it with a simple pasta tossed with olive oil and parmesan, or Horseradish Potatoes (page 245). Because the brisket is so robust, a strong vegetable like broccoli would be our choice—but probably not our children's! During the week, the remaining meat can be heated up, wrapped in a softened corn tortilla, and sprinkled with chopped tomatoes and Jack cheese. Of course, pulled shreds of warm brisket on thinly sliced rye bread with a slathering of horseradish is pretty hard to beat, too.

4½ pounds brisket of beef
Coarse salt
Coarsely ground black pepper
1 tablespoon olive oil
2 medium white onions cut, into eighths
1 medium carrot, cut into 2-inch chunks
6 flat-leaf parsley stems and some tops
¼ teaspoon crushed red pepper
2 thyme sprigs or ½ teaspoon dried thyme
1 bay leaf
3 garlic cloves, unpeeled
12 ounces dark beer
Chicken broth, preferably homemade (page 75)
1 tablespoon tomato paste

1. Rub the brisket heavily with salt and pepper. In a heavy ovenproof pan over high heat, brown the brisket in the olive oil on both sides, about 15 minutes. Remove the meat and pour off all the fat.

2. Preheat the oven to 300° F.

3. Add onions and carrot to the pan, scraping to loosen any browned bits. Stir in ½ teaspoon salt, the parsley, red pepper, thyme, bay leaf, garlic, beer, broth, and tomato paste. Bring to a boil and return the meat to the pan. Cover and place in the oven for 3 hours. Skim off fat.

4. When tender, remove the brisket to a platter and slice thinly across grain. Mash the vegetables in the pan, then press through a strainer onto the meat. The mashed vegetables will thicken and flavor the sauce.

Serves 6

Carpaccio

Like many things Italian, this dish is accompanied by a little history, controversy, and romance. Carpaccio was indeed a Venetian Renaissance painter of the fifteenth century, but whether or not he enjoyed thinly sliced raw beef for an appetizer enough times to warrant giving this delectable dish his name is unclear. The Italian term carne al carpaccio *means "beef in the style of the Carpathian Mountains," which might give a clue to the true origins of this dish.*

Carpaccio is traditionally served with very thin slices of parmesan and onion and drizzled with olive oil. (You can use a vegetable peeler or cheese slicer to cut very thin slices from a chunk of cheese.) It's a perfect first course for a special dinner for two.

6 ounces New York strip or top sirloin steak
Extra-virgin olive oil
¼ white onion, sliced paper thin
4 or 5 very thin slices parmesan
Coarse salt
¼ teaspoon coarsely ground black pepper
1 tablespoon finely chopped fresh chives

1. Chill the meat in the freezer until firm but not frozen and slice ⅛ to ¼ inch thick across the grain. Spread the work surface with 18 to 20 inches of plastic wrap and sprinkle with olive oil. Lay the slices of beef 3 inches apart and pound with the flat side of a cleaver or meat pounder. If using a cleaver, keep your wrist and hand below the level of the work surface and use a slapping motion to pound the pieces. Cover the meat with plastic wrap and refrigerate until ready to use.

2. To serve, loosely arrange 5 or 6 slices of meat to cover a plate. Sprinkle with onion and parmesan slices. Drizzle each plate with olive oil. Add salt and pepper, and sprinkle with chives.

Serves 2

The Best Burger

If you have the time to make an extra stop have your butcher grind a piece of chuck steak rather than buy already ground hamburger meat; the flavor is much superior. Like coffee beans, beef tastes best when ground immediately before using.

1½ pounds freshly ground chuck steak
Olive oil
Coarse salt
Coarsely ground black pepper
Cheddar cheese, sliced (optional)
4 hamburger buns

1. Divide the meat in four and gently press each section into a thick patty. Do not pound, knead, or squeeze it into shape; the less the meat is handled, the more tender it will be.

2. Film a cast-iron skillet with olive oil and preheat. Sprinkle both sides of the patties with salt and pepper and brown over high heat. (Burgers can, of course, also be grilled.) Cook until a crust forms and the patties become rounded on the bottom. Turn and cook until brown and crisp. Place cheese, if using, on top of each burger while the second side is cooking.

3. Meanwhile, drizzle the insides of the hamburger buns with olive oil and broil until golden brown. When the burgers are cooked, transfer them to the buns and serve immediately.

Serves 4

Veal Chops with Shiitake Mushrooms

Veal chops are so superior that they deserve a special sauce. Woodsy, meaty shiitake mushrooms complement the delicate veal without overpowering it. The meat is wonderful with Glazed Shallots (page 231) or Caramelized Red Onions (page 224).

1 tablespoon olive oil

8 fresh shiitake mushrooms, stems removed and caps thinly
  sliced

1 tablespoon finely chopped shallots

1 garlic clove, minced

1 teaspoon coarsely ground black pepper

1 cup white wine

1 cup chicken broth, preferably homemade (page 75)

1 thyme sprig

1 marjoram sprig

1 flat-leaf parsley sprig

1 sage sprig

2 tablespoons unsalted butter

1 tablespoon cognac

4 large loin veal chops

Coarse salt

Coarsely ground black pepper

¼ cup pitted and sliced green olives

1. In a skillet heat the olive oil and brown the sliced mushroom caps. Add the shallots, garlic, pepper, wine, and broth. Tie together the herb sprigs into a bouquet garni and add. Reduce over moderate heat to 1 cup. Stir in the butter and cognac. Set the sauce aside.

2. Prepare a barbecue grill.

3. Sprinkle the veal chops with salt and pepper and grill over hot coals for approximately 7 minutes on each side. Remove to a platter and keep warm.

4. Reheat the sauce in a saucepan and remove the bouquet garni. Add the olives and pour over the chops.

Serves 4

Note: The sauce can be made a day ahead, refrigerated, and reheated slowly.

Stuffed Breast of Veal

Breast of veal is an inexpensive yet tender cut of meat that adapts well to an herb flavoring. Very French! Serve the veal with small boiled potatoes and baby carrots. It can also be served cold with Aïoli (page 132) and a green salad. If you purchase a boned breast, you can slice and pack it for a picnic.

One 3- to 3½-pound breast of veal

STUFFING
1 pound ground veal
½ pound ground pork
½ onion, finely chopped
**2 teaspoons finely chopped fresh thyme or 1 teaspoon dried
     thyme**
**1½ teaspoons chopped fresh rosemary or 1 teaspoon dried
     rosemary**
8 medium garlic cloves, minced
**3 cups ½-inch bread cubes made from toasted whole-grain
     bread**
2 teaspoons coarse salt
1 teaspoon coarsely ground white pepper

2 tablespoons olive oil
1 cup chicken broth, preferably homemade (page 75)
2 cups white wine
2 garlic cloves
2 thyme sprigs or ½ teaspoon dried thyme
1 rosemary sprig or ½ teaspoon dried rosemary
½ teaspoon whole peppercorns
One 14-ounce can whole tomatoes, chopped, with liquid

1. Preheat the oven to 350° F.
2. At the large end of the veal, separate the loose top flap of meat
from the bone with a wooden spoon. Do not detach the meat at the
thinner end. With a sharp knife remove the membrane from the bottom.

3. In a medium bowl mix together the ground veal, pork, onion, thyme, rosemary, minced garlic, bread cubes, 1½ teaspoons salt, and ½ teaspoon pepper. Stuff the breast cavity with this mixture. Thread a bamboo skewer through the end to close it. Salt and pepper the outside of the veal.

4. In an ovenproof skillet large enough for the veal to fit comfortably, heat the olive oil and brown the veal on all sides. Remove from the pan and set aside. Wipe out the skillet and pour in the chicken broth and wine. Return the veal to the pan and add the garlic cloves, thyme, rosemary, peppercorns, and tomatoes. Place the pan in the oven and bake for 2 hours 30 minutes, until lightly browned and tender when pierced with a fork.

5. Remove the veal to a carving board and allow to stand for 15 to 20 minutes before serving. (The veal may also be served at room temperature.) Slice between the bones to make 1-inch-wide servings. If desired, the juices left in the pan may be strained, skimmed of fat, returned to the pan, and reduced slightly to be used as a sauce.

Serves 8

Marinated Leg of Lamb

A boned and butterflied leg of lamb has little waste and is easy to carve. This pungent marinade cuts the lamb's gaminess, and gives it a beautiful dark, almost caramelized outside.

One 5½- to 6-pound boned and butterflied leg of lamb
3 large garlic cloves, minced
3 shallots, finely chopped
¼ cup finely chopped fresh gingerroot
¼ teaspoon crushed red pepper
1 tablespoon coarsely ground black pepper
¼ cup lime juice
½ cup vegetable oil
¼ cup soy sauce
1 tablespoon honey

1. Trim the excess fat and membranes from the lamb and place it in a glass or plastic container.

2. In a small bowl mix together the garlic, shallots, ginger, red pepper, black pepper, lime juice, and ¼ cup of the vegetable oil. In a small saucepan over low heat warm the soy sauce and honey until blended. Stir into the mixture in the bowl. Pour this marinade over the lamb and turn it to coat both sides. Cover with plastic wrap and refrigerate overnight. Bring to room temperature before cooking.

3. Preheat the oven to 425° F.

4. On top of the stove over high heat, heat the remaining ¼ cup vegetable oil in a large heavy roasting pan. Place the meat in the pan, smooth side down. Sear until well browned, then turn over to brown the other side. Place in the oven and roast for 20 to 25 minutes for medium rare to rare lamb. Remove from the pan to a cutting board and allow to rest 5 minutes before carving.

Serves 8

Note: The lamb could also be barbecued. The total grilling time would be about 35 to 40 minutes. Turn the meat occasionally.

Leg of Lamb, The Best

This recipe calls for a bundle, a heap, an enormous bouquet of that ever-traditional serve-with-lamb herb, rosemary. Even if the rosemary didn't impart a wonderful flavor to the meat, the intoxicating aroma coming from the oven would be reason enough to use it in this quantity. Serve the lamb with Baba Ghanoosh (recipe follows).

Have the butcher remove the small bone from the leg of lamb to make slicing it easier.

One 4½-pound leg of lamb
3 large garlic cloves, thinly sliced
Olive oil
Coarse salt
Coarsely ground black pepper
6 ounces rosemary sprigs (8 bunches)

1. Trim off any excess fat from the meat, leaving a thin layer. Make 1-inch slits all over the meat and insert the garlic slices. Rub the lamb well with olive oil and coat heavily with salt and pepper. Wrap securely with plastic wrap and set aside for several hours, or refrigerate overnight.

2. Preheat the oven to 500° F.

3. Heat an ovenproof skillet or heavy pan large enough for the lamb to fit in comfortably and brown it on all sides. Remove the lamb to a platter and pour off all but 1 tablespoon of fat. Cover the bottom of pan with a bed of rosemary and place the lamb on top. Cover the lamb with more rosemary.

4. Place in the oven. After 20 minutes turn the heat down to 375° F. Roast for another 40 minutes. Remove the pan from the oven.

5. When ready to serve, take outside, carefully ignite the rosemary on top of the lamb, and allow to burn itself out. Make sure you have a tight-fitting lid handy to extinguish the flames. Brush off the woody stems. The charred rosemary imparts even more flavor to the lamb. Let it rest 10 to 15 minutes and transfer to a serving platter.

Serves 6 to 8

Note: If fresh rosemary is unavailable, soak 3 ounces of dried rosemary in water to cover for 30 minutes. Drain. Pat wet rosemary on the lamb before placing it in the oven. Do not attempt to flame it.

Baba Ghanoosh

Eggplant is one of our favorite vegetables, and this Middle Eastern dish is one of its simplest preparations. As a bed on which to lay tender slices of roast leg of lamb it is superb. It is also delicious cold, spread on homemade Croutons (page 86) as an appetizer.

1 medium unblemished eggplant (about 1½ pounds)
1 garlic clove, minced
2 tablespoons olive oil
½ teaspoon coarse salt
½ teaspoon coarsely ground black pepper
1 teaspoon lemon juice

1. Place a cast-iron skillet large enough for the eggplant to fit comfortably over high heat and put the eggplant in it. Cook for about 1 hour, carefully turning the eggplant every 15 minutes as the skin becomes black and charred. Remove from the heat and set aside until cool enough to handle.

2. Trim off the stem end of the eggplant and cut in half lengthwise. Carefully scrape out the insides with a spoon, discarding the charred skin. Some of the pulp may have darkened; this will give the eggplant a roasted flavor. Mash the pulp in a bowl with a fork, breaking up any large pieces. Stir in the garlic, olive oil, salt, pepper, and lemon juice. Let stand at room temperature for several hours or refrigerate overnight.

Serves 4 as a side dish

Lamb Stew

This very flavorful stew can be ready in just one hour. Serve it in bowls with a thick slice of crusty rosemary or other herb bread in the bottom.

3 pounds boneless lamb stew meat, trimmed of fat and cut
   into 1½-inch cubes
Coarse salt
Coarsely ground black pepper
4 tablespoons olive oil
2 large onions, cut into eighths
1 cup white wine
½ cup tarragon vinegar
1 cup chicken broth, preferably homemade (page 75)
1 large rosemary sprig or 1 teaspoon dried rosemary
1 bay leaf
1 thyme sprig or 1 teaspoon dried thyme
6 parsley sprigs
4 garlic cloves
12 ounces fresh spinach, washed and stemmed

1. Sprinkle the lamb with salt and pepper. In a large heavy sauté pan over medium heat brown the meat on all sides in 2 tablespoons of the olive oil. Remove from the pan. Pour the remaining olive oil into the pan and add the onions. Cook over medium heat until the onions are softened. Stir in the wine, vinegar, broth, herbs, and garlic. Return the meat to the pan, cover, and simmer for 40 minutes, until tender.

2. Remove the lamb and set aside. Skim off the fat. Pour the contents of the pan through a strainer into another pan, pressing on the sides of the strainer with a rubber spatula. Discard what is left in the strainer. Add the lamb to the pan and bring to a simmer. Add the spinach and cook just until it wilts. Serve with Mashed Potatoes with Parsley Root (page 241).

Serves 4 to 6

Lamb Chops
in Pomegranate Marinade

The intense magenta color of pomegranate juice stains the lamb chops so that when they are broiled or grilled the outside turns burgundy. This marinade can also be used for a boneless leg of lamb. To juice a pomegranate, cut it in half through the stem end and press over a reamer or electric juicer. If pomegranates are not in season, you can buy bottled pomegranate juice in a Middle Eastern or Armenian market.

¼ cup olive oil
4 garlic cloves, finely chopped
1 tablespoon chopped fresh marjoram or 1 teaspoon dried
    marjoram
1 tablespoon chopped fresh thyme or 1 teaspoon dried thyme
1 tablespoon whole black peppercorns, cracked
2 tablespoons chopped fresh flat-leaf parsley
½ cup dry red wine
½ cup pomegranate juice
8 loin or rib lamb chops

1. In a small saucepan heat the oil over medium heat, add the garlic, herbs, and pepper, and cook until the herbs have softened. Add the wine and pomegranate juice and simmer for 5 minutes. Remove from the heat and cool.

2. Dip the chops in the marinade and arrange in a single layer in a glass or ceramic dish. Pour over the remaining marinade. The chops do not have to be submerged. Cover the dish and refrigerate overnight or for at least 8 hours.

3. When ready to cook, let the chops come to room temperature. Grill or broil the chops about 4 minutes per side, depending on thickness. Baste with the remaining marinade.

Serves 4

Homemade Applesauce

Hot or cold, applesauce is comfort food in its simplest form. This pale pink applesauce should be on your winter dinner menu to go with pork chops or a pork roast. But also save some for breakfast to serve over Potato Pancakes (page 27) instead of the caramelized apples.

6 pounds red apples, unpeeled and quartered
8 whole black peppercorns
2 whole cloves
3 tablespoons sugar
¼ teaspoon ground cinnamon
2 teaspoons lemon juice

1. Place the apples in a large deep pot and add water just until you can see it through the apples. Add the peppercorns and cloves and bring to a boil over medium heat. Reduce the heat to a simmer and cook, stirring every 15 minutes, until the apples are very soft and the liquid has evaporated, about 1 hour.

2. Press the apples through a coarse strainer, food mill, or ricer. Discard the skins, peppercorns, cloves, and residue in strainer.

3. Return the applesauce to the pot over low heat and add the sugar, cinnamon, and lemon juice. Warm slowly just to melt the sugar. Adjust the sugar and/or lemon juice if necessary to taste. Serve warm or chilled.

Makes 6 cups

Marinated Pork Chops with Red Cabbage

We have found that soaking any pork cut in brine (recipe follows) definitely keeps the meat moister. In this recipe the combination of searing and baking also increases tenderness.

4 double pork chops
Brine for Pork (recipe follows)
6 tablespoons balsamic vinegar
6 tablespoons chopped shallots
3 tablespoons olive oil
4 cups shredded red cabbage (about 1 pound)
¼ teaspoon coarse salt
1 tablespoon finely chopped fresh sage or 2 teaspoons dried
      sage
½ cup beef broth
2 tablespoons large capers
2 tablespoons chopped fresh flat-leaf parsley

1. Soak the pork chops in the brine overnight.

2. The next day, remove the chops and pat dry. Place in a shallow ceramic or glass container and pour on 4 tablespoons of the balsamic vinegar with 2 tablespoons of the shallots. Cover and marinate at room temperature for several hours.

3. Preheat the oven to 450° F.

4. In a large ovenproof pan heat 1 tablespoon of the oil and sear the chops over high heat until browned. Place the pan in oven and roast the chops for 20 to 25 minutes.

5. Meanwhile, heat the remaining 2 tablespoons oil in a skillet and sauté the red cabbage with the salt and remaining 2 tablespoons balsamic vinegar. Stir in the sage and cook until the cabbage wilts. Add the remaining shallots and the beef broth and cook for about 15 minutes, until the cabbage is tender but still crunchy. Add the capers.

6. When the pork chops are done, remove to a platter and serve on a bed of cooked cabbage. Sprinkle with parsley.

Serves 4

Brine for Pork

Soaking any pork roast, bones or not, overnight in a flavorful brine will tenderize it immeasurably. Because no acid is used, the seasonings will be absorbed without the meat fiber breaking down and becoming too soft.

2 quarts water
⅓ cup coarse salt
¼ cup sugar
1 teaspoon dried thyme
3 bay leaves
5 whole cloves
10 juniper berries, crushed
1 teaspoon anise seed
1 teaspoon black peppercorns, crushed

1. In a large stockpot bring the water, salt, sugar, thyme, bay leaves, cloves, juniper berries, anise seed, and peppercorns to a boil. Reduce the heat and simmer for 15 minutes. Remove from the heat and cool to room temperature.

2. Add the pork, cover, and refrigerate overnight, or at least 12 hours. Remove the pork from the brine and pat dry. Discard the brine.

Boneless Pork Roast
with Coriander-Pepper Crust

Loin of pork is thick but tender and moist. You can soak the pork overnight in brine (page 219) to make sure it is succulent. Serve this with potatoes and Homemade Applesauce (page 216).

2½ to 3 pounds boneless pork loin
½ cup fresh bread crumbs
¼ teaspoon cayenne
1 teaspoon coarsely ground black pepper
1½ teaspoons whole coriander seeds
2 teaspoons coarse salt
1 large garlic clove
2 tablespoons olive oil

1. Using a mortar and pestle make a paste of the bread crumbs, cayenne, pepper, coriander seeds, salt, and garlic. You can also use a mini-chopper, but add the garlic last. Rub the paste well onto all sides of the meat. Wrap in plastic wrap and refrigerate overnight or leave at room temperature for several hours. When ready to cook, bring to room temperature if the pork has been refrigerated.

2. Preheat the oven to 400° F.

3. Heat the olive oil in a large ovenproof skillet over high heat. Brown the pork quickly on all sides and place in the oven. Roast for 30 minutes. Remove from the oven and allow to stand for 10 minutes before slicing.

Serves 4 to 6

Slow-cooked Pork

The secret of this richly seasoned and aromatic dish is long slow cooking. As the flavors meld, the meat becomes so tender it literally falls apart. Our kids like this because it reminds them of Mexican fast food.

4 slices thick-cut bacon, cut into ½-inch pieces
3½ pounds boneless pork shoulder or butt, trimmed of fat and
    cut into 2-inch pieces
3½ teaspoons ground cumin
3½ teaspoons ground coriander
1½ teaspoons coarse salt
2 teaspoons coarsely ground black pepper
1 cup red wine vinegar
1 tablespoon honey
1 large white onion, cut into eighths
6 large garlic cloves, chopped
¼ teaspoon crushed red pepper
1 fresh jalapeño pepper, finely chopped
3 thyme sprigs or ½ teaspoon dried thyme
½ cup beef broth
½ cup water
12 flour tortillas (6 inches each)

GARNISH
2 small tomatoes, chopped
1 avocado, peeled and sliced
¼ cup coarsely chopped cilantro
1 jalapeño, minced

1. In a heavy 12-inch skillet or shallow pan sauté the bacon and drain on paper towels. Pour off all the fat and return 3 tablespoons to the pan. Add the pork to the pan with the bacon fat, and toss with cumin, coriander, salt, and pepper. Over high heat brown the meat well on all sides. Cook in batches if necessary, as the meat will not brown well when crowded.

2. In a small saucepan stir together the vinegar and honey, bring to a boil over medium heat, and reduce to ½ cup. Pour over the meat in the pan and add the onion, garlic, red pepper, jalapeño, and thyme. Scraping the bottom of pan, mix all the ingredients together, lower the heat, cover, and simmer for 1 hour 30 minutes. Add the beef broth and water and continue cooking for another 30 minutes. The meat should be tender and caramelized, with only a little liquid left in the pan.

3. Remove from the heat and pull apart into smaller chunks with 2 forks. Serve in warmed flour tortillas topped with tomatoes, avocado, cilantro, and jalapeño.

Serves 6

Vegetables

As kids growing up in the sixties, many of us hated vegetables, probably because they were canned or frozen. Our children can't use that excuse for not liking vegetables, but they still manage to come up with a few, especially when it comes to trying some of the stronger-tasting ones, like onions or Brussels sprouts. Carrots, corn, potatoes, and milder green vegetables like zucchini are what they generally prefer.

Actually, once our daughter, Vanessa, decided to stop eating meat, she became much more adventurous about vegetables. Her decision surprised us, but since it was a personal one and not because of any peer pressure, we do respect it. For family dinners, the rest of us still enjoy meat sometimes, but we make sure that there are enough vegetables for Vanessa, along with rice or other grains, beans, or pasta. She has recently discovered artichokes, and asks us to prepare them for her very often.

These days, all of us in the family find ourselves eating more vegetables than ever before, which is good considering that nutritionists are now recommending that everyone eat at least five servings a day of vegetables and fruit. The truth is, today's kids are really much luckier than we were in the sixties. Never before has such a variety of fresh produce been available in supermarkets all across America. There's really no excuse for not liking vegetables.

But first you have to start with fresh—really fresh—vegetables. If you can get great produce at your local grocery, fine. If not, search out farmers' markets or think about growing vegetables in your backyard. There is nothing like the pleasure of going out into your own garden, picking a red ripe tomato, and biting into it on the spot.

Next, you have to cook vegetables as quickly and lightly as possible. For example, zucchini, abundantly and perennially available, needs only to be split and grilled to land on your plate in eight minutes. Onions, potatoes, and fennel can be roasted whole. Spinach and other greens can be stir-fried in a few minutes. Consider how little a vegetable needs to be altered to be enjoyed and choose your cooking method accordingly.

Caramelized Red Onions

Red onions have a sweetness all their own. When baked with balsamic vinegar, they caramelize for a delicious hot or cold accompaniment to grilled meats or fish.

3 medium red onions
2 tablespoons olive oil
3 tablespoons balsamic vinegar

1. Preheat the oven to 400° F.
2. Cut each onion into sixths, leaving the root end attached.
3. In a nonstick ovenproof pan heat the olive oil over high heat. Place the onion wedges cut side down and brown (this side only). Sprinkle with balsamic vinegar. Bake for 15 to 20 minutes, until the juices in the pan are dark and syrupy. Serve immediately or let cool in the juices and chill.

Serves 6

Baked Acorn Squash with Garlic

Acorn squash is a colorful and nutritious addition to the dinner plate that most children love. If the squash are large, cut them into smaller, more manageable pieces after baking. Toppings can be varied. You could fill the cavity with honey, nutmeg, and butter; or you could use finely diced bacon and when the squash is done, sprinkle it with parmesan cheese and run it under the broiler for three minutes.

2 acorn squash
4 tablespoons olive oil
3 garlic cloves, finely chopped
1 teaspoon coarse salt
¼ teaspoon coarsely ground black pepper
½ teaspoon dried thyme

1. Preheat the oven to 400° F.

2. Cut each squash in half through the stem end. Scrape out the seeds and loose fibers. Drizzle each half with 1 tablespoon of the olive oil and sprinkle with garlic, salt, pepper, and thyme. Place the squash on a baking sheet in the center of the oven and bake for 1 hour, or until the pulp is very soft.

3. Remove to a serving platter and let rest 5 minutes to allow the seasonings to be absorbed. Cut each half in half or thirds, if desired.

Serves 4 to 6

Roasted Fennel

We've tasted fennel in dishes from appetizers to desserts. Here we simply roast it and melt some parmesan on top. There is a natural affinity between fennel and fish, especially the milder kinds like sole, snapper, and sea bass. Roast the fennel first so your last-minute attention can be focused on the fish.

2 fennel bulbs, trimmed and sliced lengthwise ¼ inch thick
½ teaspoon coarse salt
¼ teaspoon coarsely ground black pepper
3 tablespoons olive oil
1 cup chicken broth, preferably homemade (page 75)
½ cup grated parmesan

1. Preheat the oven to 375° F.
2. Lay the fennel slices, slightly overlapping, in a 9 × 13-inch pan. Sprinkle with salt and pepper, and drizzle with olive oil. Carefully pour chicken broth around the edges. The liquid should come a quarter of the way up. Cover the pan tightly with foil and bake for 45 minutes, or until the slices feel soft.
3. Remove from the oven and sprinkle with parmesan. Place under the broiler just until the cheese melts.

Serves 4

Sautéed Spinach

If small, tender spinach leaves are unavailable, cut or tear larger leaves into smaller pieces. Sautéed spinach is the vegetable component in Nancy's favorite meal of Peppered Steak (page 201).

1¼ pounds fresh young spinach
2 tablespoons olive oil
1 tablespoon unsalted butter
¼ cup minced onion
1 anchovy fillet, crushed with a fork

1. Wash the spinach in several changes of water and remove the stems. Dry thoroughly on paper towels or use a salad spinner.

2. In a large skillet or other pan heat the oil and butter and sauté the onion over medium heat until soft. Add the anchovy fillet and sauté another 30 seconds. Add the spinach and lightly stir to heat through and wilt the leaves. Toss with a fork to incorporate the onion and anchovy and remove to a serving dish. Serve immediately.

Serves 4

Sautéed Zucchini Halves

A very simple, very fast, and very delicious way to prepare zucchini. Our children love this.

6 small or medium zucchini, cut lengthwise, then in half
    across (about 1¼ pounds)
Coarse salt
Coarsely ground black pepper
2 tablespoons olive oil

1. Sprinkle the cut side of each zucchini with salt and pepper.

2. In a medium skillet heat the olive oil over high heat and place zucchini, cut side down, in a single layer. Sauté until golden brown, then turn over and sauté briefly on the other side. Serve immediately.

Serves 4 to 6

Variations: Brush the zucchini halves with olive oil and grill for approximately 5 minutes over hot coals, cut side down first. Flip over and grill about 3 minutes on the other side.

Place the zucchini, cut side up, 3 inches from the heat of an oven broiler. Turn when well browned, 5 to 6 minutes, and cook another 3 minutes.

Oven-baked Tomato Halves

Whatever tomatoes are in season are the ones to use here. Italian plum tomatoes are our first choice. Whole cherry tomatoes can also be used. The tomatoes need to be completely cooled before they are removed from the pan, so prepare them early in the day. Because they are sweet-tasting with a hint of herbs, these tomatoes go equally well with Seafood Salad (page 107) and Broiled Marinated Chicken (page 187). For a light lunch, toss the tomatoes with pasta dressed with olive oil.

2 pounds plum or other medium tomatoes (about 12)
3 tablespoons olive oil
2 teaspoons finely chopped garlic
1 tablespoon chopped fresh rosemary or 2 teaspoons dried
    rosemary
1 tablespoon chopped fresh thyme or 1 teaspoon dried thyme
½ teaspoon coarse salt
½ teaspoon coarsely ground black pepper
1 tablespoon sugar

1. Preheat the oven to 300° F.

2. Cut the tomatoes in half through the stem end. In a medium bowl stir together the oil, garlic, herbs, salt, pepper, and sugar. Add the tomatoes and toss to coat.

3. Lay the tomatoes, cut side down, on a baking sheet. Bake for 30 minutes, until shriveled on top and caramelized on the bottom. Let cool completely before removing from the pan.

Tomatoes serve 6 as a side dish; or, tossed with 1 pound of pasta, can serve 4 as a main dish or 6 as a side dish

Glazed Shallots

Shallots are delicious with grilled or roasted meats, accompanied perhaps by potatoes or carrots. They can be added to Onion Soup (page 85) for a tender surprise bite at the bottom of the bowl. Sliced shallots add a sweet grace note to sandwiches.

2 tablespoons olive oil
12 medium shallots, peeled (1 pound)
Coarse salt
1 bay leaf
¼ teaspoon dried savory
2 thyme sprigs or ¼ teaspoon dried thyme
¾ cup white wine
¼ cup chicken broth, preferably homemade (page 75)
¼ teaspoon coarsely ground black pepper
¼ cup chopped fresh flat-leaf parsley

1. Heat the olive oil in a medium saucepan and add the shallots. Spread out in a single layer. Cook over high heat, turning to brown on all sides, about 5 minutes. Add a pinch of salt, the bay leaf, savory, thyme, wine, and chicken broth and reduce the heat to low. Cover and cook until the shallots are tender, 20 to 30 minutes, depending on size.

2. Remove the shallots with a slotted spoon and set aside. Remove the bay leaf and thyme sprig and discard. Bring the liquid left in the saucepan to a boil and reduce by half. Return the shallots to the pan and toss to glaze on all sides. Sprinkle with pepper and parsley.

Serves 4 to 6

Grilled Skewered Vegetables

Grilling vegetables on two bamboo skewers makes turning them easier and prevents pieces from falling through the rack. Keep like vegetables together because cooking times will vary, and you'll want to remove each vegetable from the grill as soon as it is done. This also allows children to pick their favorite vegetables—usually zucchini or potato—from among the skewers without the risk of commingling with an unfavorite vegetable—like scallions or mushrooms.

Use any of the vegetables listed, in any quantity you like.

Zucchini, cut into ½-inch-thick rounds and parboiled for 1 minute

Russet potatoes, unpeeled, cut into ½-inch-thick rounds and parboiled for 10 minutes

Yams, unpeeled, cut into ½-inch-thick rounds and parboiled for 10 minutes

Japanese or regular eggplants, unpeeled, cut into ½-inch-thick rounds

Sweet onions, such as Maui or Vidalia, or regular onions, cut into ½-inch-thick rounds

Scallions, trimmed to 6 inches

White or shiitake mushroom caps

Olive oil

Coarse salt

Coarsely ground black pepper

1. Prepare a barbecue grill. Soak bamboo skewers in water for 30 minutes while the grill is heating up.

2. Lay the vegetable pieces on a work surface and insert 2 parallel skewers into each piece to resemble a lollipop. More than 1 piece may be threaded on each set of skewers. As many as 4 scallions can be threaded through the white part on 2 skewers. Keep like vegetables together. Brush both sides of the vegetables with olive oil and sprinkle with salt and pepper.

3. Grill about 4 inches from the hot coals, turning and basting once with oil, taking care not to burn them. Scallions will take 2 to 4 minutes; yams about 12 minutes; eggplant, potatoes, and onions about 15.

Braised Bitter Greens

For bitter greens, you can usually find dandelion, mustard, or turnip greens or broccoli rabe. Taste a piece before cooking. If very bitter, blanch the greens in boiling water for fifteen seconds and squeeze dry before braising. Select young leaves without fibrous stems and buy only as much as you can use immediately, as greens do not store well.

4 strips thick-sliced bacon, cut into 1-inch pieces
1¼ pounds bitter greens
Crushed red pepper
½ cup water

1. In a large nonreactive skillet or saucepan sauté the bacon until the fat is rendered and the bacon is lightly browned. Remove with a slotted spoon and set aside on paper towels.

2. Wash the greens and remove the stems. Put in the pan with the bacon fat and add the red pepper and water. Cover and turn the heat to low. Cook for 10 to 12 minutes, until the greens are tender. Toss with the bacon and serve.

Serves 4

Pan-charred Broccoli in Hot Chili Oil

Serve this with a mild white fish, such as halibut, sole, or snapper.

2 pounds broccoli
⅓ cup olive oil
⅓ cup chicken broth, preferably homemade (page 75)
2 garlic cloves, minced
¼ teaspoon coarse salt
¼ teaspoon crushed red pepper
Juice of ½ lemon

1. Cut the broccoli into 2-inch-long florets. Peel the outer layer from the broccoli stalks and cut into julienne strips about 2 inches long.

2. In a large sauté pan heat 1 tablespoon of the olive oil until smoking and place all the broccoli pieces in one layer and sauté for 30 seconds. Pour in the broth, garlic, and salt, and immediately cover the pan. Remove from the heat and leave to steam for 2 minutes.

3. Meanwhile, in a small saucepan heat the remaining olive oil with the red pepper. Pour over the broccoli, tossing to coat well. Squeeze fresh lemon juice over all and serve.

Serves 6

Roasted Onions
with Mustard Vinaigrette

Onions are always on hand in our kitchen, and this is our favorite way to prepare them. Delicious with a simple grilled steak or fish fillet.

2 very large red onions or 4 medium white onions,
     dry outer skin peeled
2 tablespoons olive oil
1 teaspoon coarse salt

VINAIGRETTE
2 tablespoons lemon juice
1 teaspoon chopped fresh thyme or ½ teaspoon dried thyme
1 teaspoon Dijon mustard
¼ teaspoon coarsely ground black pepper
¼ cup extra-virgin olive oil

1. Preheat the oven to 375° F.

2. If using very large red onions, cut them in half through the stem end and place them, cut side down, in a shallow pan just large enough to hold them. If using smaller white onions, slice a small piece off the stem end so that they can stand up. Cut an **X** into the top of the white onions, about ½ inch deep. Drizzle onions with olive oil and sprinkle with salt. Bake, uncovered, for 1 hour to 1 hour 30 minutes, basting several times with any juices that have accumulated. When done, the onions will feel soft to the touch in the center and will look lightly browned and caramelized. They will come apart somewhat.

3. Prepare the vinaigrette by stirring together the lemon juice, thyme, mustard, and pepper. Gradually whisk in the oil. The mixture will not become emulsified. Pour over the onions and serve.

Serves 4

Brussels Sprouts with Crisped Garlic

This is a novel way to serve Brussels sprouts—just barely cooked and dressed in a light vinaigrette. When cooking the garlic, be careful not to burn the thin slices; they can easily turn bitter. Also to avoid a bitter taste, remove the green center of each clove if present.

1¼ pounds Brussels sprouts, as small as possible
1 large head garlic, separated into cloves, peeled
2 tablespoons olive oil

VINAIGRETTE
1½ tablespoons white wine vinegar
½ tablespoon lemon juice
½ teaspoon Dijon mustard
¼ teaspoon coarsely ground black pepper
¼ teaspoon coarse salt
½ teaspoon chopped fresh thyme or ¼ teaspoon dried thyme
½ cup extra-virgin olive oil

Greens or lettuce for serving

1. Cut a small slice from the stem end of each of the Brussels sprouts and remove any tough outer leaves. Bring a large pot of salted water to a boil; add the sprouts, and cook just until their color brightens and the inside feels tender when cut in half. Drain and immediately plunge into a bowl of ice water. When completely cool, drain and cut in half (if large, cut into quarters).

2. Thinly slice each garlic clove. Fry the garlic in olive oil over low heat, stirring constantly. When done, the slices will be very sticky and the color of toast. Discard any that are too brown. Drain and separate on paper towels.

3. In a medium bowl whisk together the vinegar, lemon juice, mustard, pepper, salt, and thyme. Slowly whisk in the olive oil until emulsified. Arrange the greens on a serving platter. Toss the Brussels sprouts with the vinaigrette and mound on the greens. Sprinkle with crisped garlic slices.

Serves **6**

Peas with Shallots and Prosciutto

Good fresh peas are essential to the success of this dish.

2 cups shelled peas (3 pounds in the pod)
1 tablespoon unsalted butter
1 small shallot, finely minced
3 slices prosciutto, cut into julienne (about 1½ ounces)
Coarse salt
Coarsely ground black pepper

  1. Boil the peas in lightly salted water for 4 to 5 minutes, until they no longer taste starchy but are still firm. Drain.
  2. In the same pan melt the butter and add the drained peas, shallot, and prosciutto. Toss lightly to warm through. Season to taste with salt and pepper.

Serves 4

Black Beans

This is a hearty side dish that goes well with grilled sausages for a simple, satisfying supper.

1 pound dried black beans, soaked in water to cover overnight
½ large onion, cut into eighths
3 garlic cloves, sliced
1 tablespoon olive oil
¾ pound smoked ham hock
2 cups chicken broth, preferably homemade (page 75)
3 cups water
1 teaspoon coarse salt
1 teaspoon coarsely ground black pepper
¼ teaspoon crushed red pepper
One 28-ounce can whole tomatoes with their liquid

GARNISH
¼ cup finely chopped onions
1 jalapeño, seeded and finely chopped
½ cup coarsely chopped cilantro
½ cup sour cream

1. Rinse the beans in 3 changes of water and pick through to remove any stones. In a large soup pot over high heat sauté the onion and garlic in the olive oil just until lightly browned. Add the ham hock, broth, water, salt, pepper, red pepper, tomatoes, and beans. Stir together, breaking up the tomatoes with a spoon, bring to a boil, then lower the heat, cover, and cook, stirring often, for approximately 2 hours, adding more water if the beans become dry. (The beans can also be baked at 300° F. for the same length of time.)

2. To serve, garnish with chopped onion, jalapeño, cilantro, and sour cream.

Serves 8 to 10

Tempura Onion Rings

Prepare these onion rings at the last minute to serve with a main-dish salad or cold herbed chicken. The success of the tempura method depends on dropping very cold battered vegetables into very hot oil, so keep the bowl of batter sitting in a bowl of ice cubes.

2 large sweet onions, such as Maui, Vidalia, or Spanish red
2 cups cake flour
½ cup cornstarch
½ teaspoon cayenne
1 teaspoon baking powder
2 egg whites
2½ cups ice-cold sparkling water or club soda
3 cups peanut oil

1. Remove the outer skin and ends of the onions and cut into ⅓-inch slices. Separate into rings.

2. In a large bowl mix together the flour, cornstarch, cayenne, and baking powder. In a separate bowl whisk the egg whites until foamy. Add the sparkling water to the egg whites and stir into the dry ingredients until combined but not entirely smooth. The batter will be very liquid. Set the bowl into a larger bowl full of ice cubes.

3. In a deep saucepan heat the oil to 375° F.

4. Dip several onion rings at a time into the batter and drop them into the hot oil, no more than 4 at a time. Cook until lightly browned, about 2 minutes. Turn if necessary to brown the opposite side. Remove with a slotted spoon to paper towels to drain. Keep warm in a warm oven (200° F.). Repeat until all the rings have been cooked.

Serves 6

Mashed Potatoes with Parsley Root

When blended together these two mildly flavored white root vegetables become more complex and fresher-tasting to make a splendid accompaniment to meat dishes. Look for parsley root in the fall and again at Passover. It is a small parsnip-looking vegetable with feathery parsley leaves.

1 pound russet potatoes, peeled and cut into 1-inch pieces
1 pound parsley root, peeled and cut into 1-inch pieces
5 garlic cloves, finely chopped
¾ cup heavy cream
3 tablespoons unsalted butter
2 teaspoons coarse salt
1 teaspoon coarsely ground black pepper

GARNISH
2 tablespoons chopped fresh flat-leaf parsley

1. Place the potatoes and parsley root in a medium saucepan with water to cover. Bring to a boil, cover, and cook until tender, about 15 minutes. Drain.

2. In the bowl of an electric mixer combine the potatoes and parsley root with the garlic, cream, and butter. With the paddle attachment beat together on medium speed until everything is well mixed and the butter has melted. (Or mix by hand with a potato masher until the ingredients are combined but not finely pureed.) There should be some small chunks left after mixing. Add salt and pepper, adjusting the seasoning if necessary. Sprinkle with parsley.

Serves 6

Mashed Potatoes with Olive Oil and Greek Olives

This recipe is inspired by a dish Jonathan Waxman prepared for a dinner at the Parkway Grill in Pasadena. He served it with roast duck. We like it with Beef Shanks (page 198).

3 pounds russet potatoes, peeled, cut in half if large
4 tablespoons (½ stick) unsalted butter
1 cup extra-virgin olive oil
½ cup pitted and sliced oil-cured Greek olives, or Moroccan olives
1 cup milk
1¼ teaspoons coarse salt
¾ teaspoon coarsely ground pepper

1. Place the potatoes in a large saucepan with water to cover. Bring to a boil over medium heat and cook until tender, about 20 minutes. Drain.

2. Place potatoes and butter in the bowl of an electric mixer and beat with the paddle attachment until smooth, but not more than 2 minutes or they will become gummy. Some small lumps will remain. Beat in ¾ cup of the olive oil, olives, milk, salt, and pepper.

3. To serve, scoop some potatoes onto each plate and drizzle with additional olive oil.

Serves 6 to 8

Potato Shoes

Once you make these, the name will no longer be a mystery. They truly resemble the soles of shoes, shoes for very tiny feet.

3 small russet potatoes (4 to 6 ounces each)
3 tablespoons vegetable oil
Coarse salt
Coarsely ground black pepper

1. Preheat the oven to 450° F.
2. Without peeling, slice the potatoes lengthwise ½ inch thick. In an ovenproof skillet large enough to hold all the potato slices in 1 layer, heat the oil. Place the potatoes in the pan and cook over medium heat until well browned on the bottom.
3. Sprinkle with salt and pepper and place in the oven. Bake for about 20 minutes, until soft to the touch. Do not turn during cooking. Serve bottom side up.

Serves 4

Variation: The sliced potatoes may also be placed under and around a roast or leg of lamb and baked without turning.

Roasted Garlic Potatoes

When garlic is roasted, its sharp bite mellows to a nutty taste, its firmness roasts to a buttery softness. Don't be shy about combining this amount of roasted garlic with mashed potatoes; the result is ideal with a hearty meat dish.

2 large heads garlic, left whole and unpeeled
¼ cup olive oil
3 pounds russet potatoes, peeled and quartered
4 tablespoons (½ stick) unsalted butter
½ teaspoon coarse salt
½ teaspoon coarsely ground black pepper

1. Preheat the oven to 350° F.
2. Place the garlic in a small baking pan and drizzle with 2 tablespoons of the olive oil. Roast in the center of the oven for 30 to 40 minutes, until it feels soft when gently squeezed. Remove the garlic from the oven and let it cool for 15 minutes.
3. Meanwhile, place the potatoes in water to cover and boil, covered, for 30 minutes, until tender. Drain. Mash in a medium bowl with a potato masher or fork. Mix in the remaining 2 tablespoons of olive oil, the butter, salt, and pepper. Cut the garlic heads in half crosswise. Squeeze out the soft garlic into the mashed potatoes, stir to combine, and serve.

Serves 6

Horseradish Potatoes

Chunky, with their red skins left on, these pungent potatoes belong with the best steak or prime rib. Select a fresh horseradish root that is exceptionally hard and free of soft spots. Horseradish root will keep for a few weeks in the refrigerator if wrapped in a slightly damp paper towel. To grate, first remove the skin and any tough outer layer. Grate only as much as you will immediately use.

1½ **pounds tiny red potatoes, unpeeled**
⅓ **cup heavy cream, heated**
½ **teaspoon coarse salt**
¼ **teaspoon coarsely ground black pepper**
½ **cup freshly grated horseradish**

1. Place the potatoes in water to cover and boil until tender. Drain.
2. Put into the bowl of an electric mixer fitted with the paddle attachment. On low speed break up the potatoes and slowly pour in the cream. Add the salt, pepper, and horseradish. Continue mixing until everything is incorporated but the mixture is still chunky. More cream may be needed if not served immediately.

Serves 4

French Fries

It's hard to imagine a rare grilled steak without a portion of these classic potatoes nearby. They're part of Nancy's favorite meal and, we imagine, lots of others' too.

2½ pounds russet potatoes
4 cups vegetable oil
Coarse salt

1. Wash the potatoes and slice them, without peeling, about ½ inch thick. Cut each slice into strips ½ inch wide. Place in ice water as you work so the potatoes don't darken. This can be done early in the day or the night before. Cover the bowl and refrigerate.

2. In a deep heavy pan heat the oil to 300° F. Drain the potatoes and dry thoroughly. Drop the potatoes into the hot oil in small batches and cook for 2 minutes. Remove with a slotted spoon. The potatoes should be white and barely tender. Spread them on paper towels or a brown paper bag to drain and come to room temperature. This step may be completed early in the day.

3. When ready to serve, heat the oil to 375° F. Refry the potatoes in the same oil in small batches for 2 minutes, until golden brown. Remove to paper towels to drain, sprinkle with salt, and serve.

Serves 4

The Best Baked Potato

A baked potato is the quintessential American accompaniment to anything grilled. But how many really great ones have you had? Too often they are wrapped in foil to speed cooking, or, worse yet, microwaved. To prevent scorched spots and ensure even heat, bake the potatoes on a layer of salt. Top with pure, thick crème fraîche, and they cannot be improved upon.

8 medium russet potatoes (6 ounces each)
Softened unsalted butter
Coarse salt
1½ cups Crème Fraîche (recipe follows)
½ cup finely chopped fresh chives or scallions, green parts
    only

1. Preheat the oven to 400° F.
2. Scrub the potatoes, dry, and rub the skins with butter. Pour about 1½ cups of salt over the bottom of a shallow baking pan or cookie sheet, making a generous layer.
3. Lay the potatoes 2 inches apart on top of the salt and place in the oven. Bake for 50 minutes, until a potato feels tender when lightly squeezed. Remove to plates, cut open lengthwise, and fill with Crème Fraîche. Sprinkle liberally with chives and serve.

Serves 8

Crème Fraîche

Crème fraîche is excellent to have on hand for all sorts of purposes. Mark loves it on a hot baked potato, and Nancy thinks nothing is so wonderful as perfectly ripe summer fruits—berries especially—topped with a dollop of crème fraîche.

3 cups heavy cream
4 tablespoons buttermilk

Stir the cream and buttermilk together in a large bowl. Cover tightly. Let the mixture stand at room temperature for 36 hours, until slightly thickened. Refrigerate the cream for 24 hours to thicken further. Crème fraîche keeps up to 10 days in the refrigerator, continuing to thicken as it stands.

Makes 3 cups

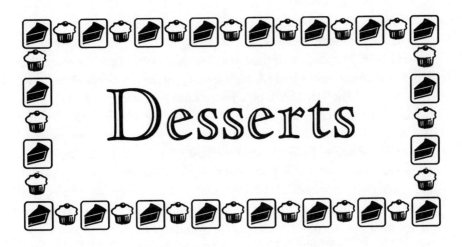

Desserts

Most weeknights, family meals at our house end with fresh fruit. Desserts are Nancy's specialty—she loves to make them, and the children love to eat them—but these days she is often so busy with the café and the bakery that they have to be reserved for special occasions and company dinners. Nancy has made the recipes in this chapter much simpler than the ones in her previous *Desserts* book. She simply doesn't have time to fuss in the kitchen with a complicated dessert, and we suspect that most home cooks don't either. For the times when you do want to serve dessert but don't want to devote hours to its preparation, these recipes are ideal.

The desserts here follow the philosophy that we have tried to emphasize throughout the book: simplicity in preparation, using only basic skills and equipment. Because of this paring down, ingredients must be the very best. The success of the Chocolate Nougatine Tart, for example, depends on using fine-flavored, high-quality bittersweet chocolate; anything less and the tart just won't be as superb as it ought to be.

Many of the recipes are variations on ideas we are all familiar with. The recipe for Individual Lattice-topped Berry Pies, for example, has only minor changes from the one for basic fruit pie: the lattice top is made in a large sheet, chilled, and cut to fit small pies for a more personal and attractive presentation. For Strawberries in Beaujolais Sauce, the berries are cooked first to release their natural juices before they are refrigerated and served, resulting in a wonderful blending of color and tastes. The Plum Rhubarb Crisp is a homey dessert in which the fruit itself is unsweetened, sweetness being derived from the streusel topping alone.

We've also limited the use of fancy pastry equipment and special pans and molds. Professional dessert chefs can rely on an endless supply of pans and utensils and, of course, a staff to help with the cooking and clean-up; the home cook doesn't have this luxury. So we've concentrated on simple desserts, like Bittersweet Chocolate Mousse and Strawberries in Beaujolais Sauce, that make use of ingredients and techniques that are manageable.

These desserts will still take more time than peeling an orange, but the extra effort is really worth it sometimes. When a main course is very, very simple, a special dessert can make your guests feel special and indulged.

Meyer Lemon Tart

The Meyer lemon, a common backyard fruit in California, has a smooth skin and an unforgettable perfume. It is sweeter than a regular lemon. Look for it in specialty markets or ask friends to give you some. If Meyer lemons are not available, the tart can be made with ordinary lemons. This recipe is from Patricia Wells's Food Lover's Guide to France. *It is perfect.*

½ recipe Pâte Sucrée (recipe follows)
1 cup blanched almonds
1 cup granulated sugar
4 large eggs, at room temperature
5 teaspoons grated lemon zest
8 tablespoons lemon juice
7 tablespoons unsalted butter, melted
1 recipe Lemon Curd (recipe follows)

1. Roll out the pastry dough ⅛ inch thick and fit into an 8-inch buttered pastry ring or tart pan. Refrigerate for about 1 hour.

2. Preheat the oven to 350° F.

3. Line the pastry shell with parchment paper or overlapping coffee filters and fill with pie weights or dried beans. Bake for 25 minutes, until lightly browned. Allow to cool. Remove the pie weights and baking paper. If the crust is not evenly colored, bake for another 5 minutes.

4. In a food processor fitted with the metal blade grind the almonds and sugar to a fine powder. In a medium bowl whisk together the almond mixture, eggs, zest, juice, and butter. Pour into the pastry shell.

5. Place in the oven, lower the temperature to 325° F., and bake for 30 minutes. The top will appear set and very lightly browned when done.

6. If desired, trim the edges of the pastry even with the filling. Serve the tart warm or at room temperature, accompanied by Lemon Curd.

Serves 6 to 8

Pâte Sucrée

This is Nancy's recipe from her Desserts *book. It is an excellent pastry for tarts.*

2¾ cups all-purpose flour
½ cup granulated sugar
½ pound (2 sticks) unsalted butter
2 egg yolks
¼ cup plus 2 tablespoons heavy cream

1. Sift the flour and sugar into the bowl of a food processor and pulse to combine. Cut the butter into tablespoon-size pieces and add to the mixture. Pulse until it resembles coarse meal.

2. In a small bowl whisk the egg yolks and ¼ cup of the cream together and add to the flour mixture. Pulse to moisten.

3. Remove from the food processor and gather the dough together with your hands. You may have to dribble on 2 extra tablespoons of cream to make the dough moist enough to hold together.

4. Form into 2 balls and wrap well in plastic. Chill for at least 2 hours or overnight.

Makes two 10-inch tart shells

Lemon Curd

3 eggs
2 egg yolks
¾ cup plus 1 tablespoon lemon juice, preferably from Meyer
    lemons
¾ cup sugar

1. Whisk the eggs and egg yolks together. Add the juice and sugar.

2. In a double boiler over simmering water cook and stir until thickened, 5 to 6 minutes. Remove from the heat, cool to room temperature, and refrigerate until firm. Use within a few days for best flavor.

Makes 1⅔ cups

Variation: If you are using standard lemons, increase the sugar to 1 cup and decrease the lemon juice to ¾ cup.

Fresh Date Tart

Dates and cream are just about a perfect combination. Fresh dates may take some searching out, but once you find them they can be kept frozen indefinitely after they ripen. If using other fruits, such as peaches, raspberries, or blueberries, there may be some custard left over.

½ recipe **Pâte Sucrée (page 252)**
¾ **pound fresh dates, or 4 peeled and sliced very ripe peaches
tossed with 2 tablespoons lemon juice, 3 to 4 cups
raspberries, or 2 cups blueberries**
4 egg yolks
¼ cup sugar
1½ cups heavy cream
1 vanilla bean, split and scraped

   1. Roll out the pastry dough ⅛ inch thick, fit it into a 10-inch buttered flan ring, and chill.
   2. Preheat the oven to 350° F.
   3. Line the pastry shell with parchment paper or overlapping coffee filters and fill with pie weights or dried beans. Bake for 30 minutes, until lightly browned.
   4. Slit the side of each date lengthwise and remove the pit. Squeeze the date carefully to slip off the skin. Pinch the dates back together to resemble their original shape. Place the dates in concentric circles about ¾ inch apart in the bottom of the tart shell. For variation, spread berries evenly over the bottom of the tart shell, or arrange peach slices in concentric circles.

5. In a small bowl whisk together the egg yolks and sugar. In a medium saucepan bring the cream with the vanilla bean to a boil. Remove and discard the vanilla bean. Pour a small amount of cream into the egg yolk mixture and whisk. Pour the mixture back into the saucepan and whisk until well combined. Carefully pour the custard over the dates.

6. Bake in the upper third of the oven for 20 minutes. Check for doneness by inserting the tip of a knife into the center of the custard. If it is still liquid, continue baking but watch carefully. The custard will break if overcooked. Serve warm.

Serves 8

Macadamia Nut Tart

½ recipe Pâte Sucrée (page 252)
6 tablespoons (loosely packed) dark brown sugar
6 tablespoons granulated sugar
¼ cup bourbon whiskey
¾ cup light corn syrup
2 tablespoons unsalted butter
1 vanilla bean, split and scraped
1 egg
2 egg yolks
½ pound toasted Macadamia nuts
⅓ cup unsweetened shredded coconut

1. Roll out the pastry and fit it into a 10-inch buttered flan ring. Place on a baking sheet and chill for at least 30 minutes before filling.

2. Preheat the oven to 350° F.

3. In a large bowl whisk together the brown sugar, granulated sugar, and bourbon. Beat in the corn syrup. The mixture will be very thick and sticky.

4. In a small saucepan over high heat melt the butter with the vanilla bean until the butter is brown and foamy. Continue heating until the bubbles subside and the butter turns dark brown and starts to smoke. It will give off a nutty aroma. Pour immediately into the sugar mixture and whisk until combined. Remove and discard the vanilla bean. Cool.

5. In another bowl whisk together the egg and egg yolks. Add to the cooled sugar mixture and beat vigorously by hand until combined.

6. Arrange the macadamia nuts evenly in the tart shell. Pour in 1½ cups of the filling. There may be some left over. Bake for 35 to 40 minutes, until the filling rises in a small dome and is uniformly brown. During the last 10 minutes of baking sprinkle the top of the tart with coconut. When done, the center of the tart will be a little soft; but if overcooked, the filling will be hard and candylike. Be careful not to overcook. Serve warm with softly whipped cream or ice cream.

Serves 8

Note: Unsweetened coconut is available in health-food stores.

Chocolate Nougatine Tart

This is a deeply chocolate flavored dessert. We recommend that you use a European bittersweet chocolate, such as Tobler or Lindt, to get the right intensity. The puddinglike filling rests on a layer of nougatine, which also seals the crust and keeps it crisp. If you use a less bitter chocolate, reduce the sugar by two tablespoons and add one ounce more of chocolate.

½ recipe Pâte Sucrée (page 252)

NOUGATINE
1 cup minus 2 tablespoons sugar
6 tablespoons water
1 cup sliced almonds
½ tablespoon unsalted butter

FILLING
2 eggs
4 egg yolks
3 tablespoons sugar
7 ounces bittersweet or extra-bittersweet chocolate, melted
Vanilla ice cream or unsweetened whipped cream

1. Roll out the pastry, fit it into a 10-inch buttered flan ring, and chill.
2. Preheat the oven to 350° F.

3. Line the shell with parchment paper or overlapping coffee filters and fill with dried beans or pie weights. Bake for 25 minutes, until golden brown. Remove the paper and beans and bake for an additional 5 minutes if the bottom isn't colored. Cool before filling.

4. To make the nougatine, stir together the sugar and water in an 8-inch skillet and bring to a boil over high heat. Brush down the sides of the pan if sugar crystals begin to form. Cook until the mixture turns a deep amber color. Remove from heat and immediately add the almonds, stirring to coat well and brown slightly. Quickly stir in the butter and pour into the tart shell. Spread the nougatine as quickly and as evenly as possible. Set aside.

5. Preheat the oven to 325° F.

6. With the whisk attachment on an electric mixer beat the eggs, egg yolks, and sugar on high speed until pale yellow and thickened, about 5 minutes. Slowly fold in the melted chocolate until completely incorporated. Pour over the nougatine and smooth the top.

7. Bake in the upper third of the oven for 5 to 6 minutes, until the filling has lost its shine. The outer 3 inches will be barely set and still sticky. Press the center lightly to test; it should be very soft. Remove from the oven and cool to room temperature.

8. The tart is best served warm, with vanilla ice cream or whipped cream, a few hours after it is made. If you hold it over to the next day, store the tart at room temperature and warm it in a 500° F. oven for 3 to 4 minutes.

Serves 8 to 10

Individual
Lattice-topped Berry Pies

This dessert is so simple—just berries mixed with a little sugar and zest, topped with a flaky latticework pastry crust—but the presentation makes it extra-special. What guest wouldn't love to have a whole little pie to himself? The latticework is easy when done this way.

FLAKY PIE DOUGH

2 cups all-purpose flour
1½ teaspoons sugar
1 teaspoon ground cinnamon
¼ teaspoon freshly grated nutmeg
⅛ teaspoon ground cloves
½ pound (2 sticks) unsalted butter
2 egg yolks
3 tablespoons heavy cream or milk

FILLING

2 cups blackberries
2 cups raspberries
4 to 5 tablespoons sugar
2 teaspoons grated orange zest
1½ tablespoons cornstarch dissolved in 3 tablespoons water
1 teaspoon water for wash
4 tablespoons sugar

Vanilla ice cream

1. In the bowl of a mixer or a food processor fitted with the metal blade combine the flour, sugar, and spices. Cut the butter into tablespoon-size pieces and mix or pulse to combine with the dry ingredients. Add the yolks and cream, mixing just until combined. The mixture will still appear dry and crumbly. Transfer the dough from the bowl to a floured board and knead lightly with the heel of your hand until it holds together. Form into a disk and wrap well in plastic wrap. Chill for at least 2 hours or overnight.

2. When ready to make the lattice, remove the dough from the refrigerator and cut it in half. Return half to the refrigerator for another use (see Note). On a floured board roll out the dough into a ¼-inch-thick rectangle 10½ × 15½ inches. Using a metal ruler, cut lengthwise into ¾-inch strips. Lay 9 strips ¼ inch apart on the back of a cookie sheet. Beginning in the center, weave in the remaining strips, piecing when necessary. Using a 4-inch round cookie cutter or the top of one of the individual pie dishes, cut out 8 rounds. Leave them in place on the cookie sheet and chill well before using.

3. To make the filling, toss together the berries, sugar, zest, and dissolved cornstarch.

4. Preheat the oven to 400° F.

5. Set out 8 individual 4-inch round, 1-inch high, fluted quiche or soufflé dishes. Divide the fruit mixture evenly among the dishes. With a wide spatula carefully lift the pastry rounds off the cookie sheet and lay on top of the fruit. Brush each lattice with water and sprinkle with 1½ teaspoons of sugar. Place the dishes in a large roasting pan filled with water to come halfway up the sides of the dishes.

6. Bake for 35 to 40 minutes. The fruit should be bubbling around the lattice and the pastry should look lightly browned and sugar-crusted. Remove from the oven and let to stand for 1 to 2 hours. Top with a scoop of vanilla ice cream before serving.

Serves 8

Note: The amount of pastry in this recipe is more than you will need for 8 individual pies because in pastry making it's always a good idea to have a little extra. That way, you won't panic if you can't get the pastry to roll out exactly right or if your first attempt at lattice-making is less than perfect. You can always use the leftover dough to make another batch of tarts or pies. The dough can be refrigerated overnight or frozen for 2 weeks.

Brioche Tart with Summer Fruit

Brioche is a bread dough rich with eggs and butter, most often formed into rolls or a loaf identified by a little topknot. It can also be baked as a tart shell with a simple rolled border. This inspired version was created by our pastry chef, Brendt Rogers. If you make the whole recipe for the dough, the second half will make twelve individual brioche rolls. Remember that brioche dough must be cold and worked with quickly.

½ recipe Brioche (recipe follows)
1 cup Crème Fraîche (page 248)
1 egg, separated
⅔ cup sugar
3 tablespoons water
1½ cups white wine
1 vanilla bean, split
3 medium peaches, peeled and thinly sliced and reserved in a
    bowl of cold water acidulated with the juice of half a
    lemon
3 apricots, pitted and quartered
¼ cup boysenberries
1 cup heavy cream, whipped

1. Line a baking sheet with parchment paper, butter a 10-inch flan ring or springform rim, and set it on the baking sheet. Set aside.

2. Pat the dough into a baseball-size ball, flatten it into a 5-inch disk, and roll it out with a rolling pin into an 11-inch circle. Take care that the edges are smooth with no cracks and use as little flour as needed to keep the dough from sticking. Ease the pastry into the ring and fold the excess dough over to make a thick rolled edge, pressing down to seal the edge to the bottom of the dough. Don't worry about making the edge perfect; the tart is supposed to have a simple, rustic look. Let rise, uncovered, in a warm place, for 2 to 3 hours, until it has risen to the top of the ring.

3. Preheat the oven to 300° F.

4. Dimple the bottom of the brioche by pressing deeply into the bottom with your fingertips.

5. In a small bowl whisk together the Crème Fraîche and egg yolk. Spread evenly over the brioche right to the edge. Brush the edges with the egg white mixed with 1 teaspoon of water and sprinkle the entire tart with ⅓ cup of the sugar. Bake in the center of the oven for 45 minutes, until golden brown. Remove and cool. Remove the flan ring and place the brioche on a serving plate.

6. In a large skillet stir together the remaining sugar, the water, and the vanilla bean. Cook over high heat without stirring. Cook until the mixture turns a medium brown and begins to smoke. Add the wine and reduce by a third. Remove the vanilla bean. Add the peaches and apricots. Cook the fruit over medium heat until glazed and translucent, about 5 minutes. If the mixture becomes dry, add a couple more tablespoons of wine. Remove from the heat. Just before serving, stir in the boysenberries. Cut the brioche into wedges and spoon the warm fruit on top. Accompany with whipped cream.

Serves 8

Brioche

1 package (¼ ounce) dry yeast
⅓ cup plus 1 tablespoon milk, heated to 100° F.
3¾ cups all-purpose flour
3 tablespoons sugar
2 teaspoons salt
2 eggs, lightly beaten
2½ sticks (10 ounces) cold unsalted butter

1. Dissolve the yeast in the milk and allow to proof for 5 minutes.

2. In the bowl of an electric mixer fitted with the paddle attachment, mix the flour, sugar, salt, and yeast mixture on low speed while adding the eggs. When the flour is uniformly moistened, add the butter by a tablespoon. This process should take about 7 to 8 minutes. The butter should be completely incorporated and the dough should begin to pull away from the sides of the bowl before the mixing process is stopped. If the dough does not clean the sides of the bowl, sprinkle on a teaspoon of flour at a time until it does.

3. Remove the dough from the bowl, form into a ball, and place in a clean bowl. Cover tightly with plastic wrap and refrigerate at least 24 hours or up to 3 days.

Makes 2 pounds

Brandied Cherries for Ice Cream

Although a little awkward to eat, unpitted cherries retain their shape and stand up to cooking. Black pepper may seem unusual in a dessert, but don't be tempted to leave it out; the pepper deepens the flavor and takes just a little edge off the sweetness.

1½ to 2 pounds fresh Bing cherries
10 tablespoons unsalted butter
¼ cup sugar
½ cup brandy
¼ teaspoon coarsely ground black pepper
2 tablespoons lemon juice
1 teaspoon pure vanilla extract

GARNISH
1 pint vanilla ice cream
2 teaspoons grated lemon zest

1. Wash the cherries and remove the stems but do not pit.

2. In a medium skillet melt 8 tablespoons of the butter with the sugar over high heat. When the mixture is foamy and golden, add the cherries and stir to coat. Reduce the heat and cook for 5 to 7 minutes. Add the brandy, ignite, and let it burn off. Add the pepper, lemon juice, and vanilla. Cover and simmer for 5 minutes. The cherries will look translucent when done. With a slotted spoon, carefully remove the cherries to a bowl.

3. Turn up the heat under the liquid and reduce until thickened and syrupy. Cut the remaining 2 tablespoons of butter into small pieces and stir into the sauce. Return the cherries to the skillet, turning to coat.

4. To serve, pour the hot cherry mixture over scoops of vanilla ice cream and sprinkle with grated lemon zest.

Serves **6**

Plum Bundles

These fragile little pastry packages that enclose a plum compote and sit in a swirl of plum sauce never fail to evoke gasps of delight from dinner guests. Don't be afraid of phyllo dough; once you get the hang of it, it's very easy to work with. Just be sure to use it as soon as possible after defrosting and to keep the unused sheets under a moist towel to prevent their drying out.

We sometimes substitute apricots or pitted fresh cherries for the plums. Although the apricot bundles turn out a little less juicy than the plum ones, they are equally delicious.

1 cup water
¾ cup granulated sugar
12 ripe but firm red plums, unpeeled, pitted and cut into
    eighths
1 vanilla bean, split and scraped
½ cup brandy
½ cup fine bread crumbs, toasted
½ teaspoon freshly grated nutmeg
1 teaspoon ground cinnamon
12 sheets frozen phyllo dough, defrosted
3 tablespoons unsalted butter, melted
¼ teaspoon pure almond extract
Homemade Yogurt (page 35)
Confectioners' sugar for dusting

1. In a medium saucepan bring the water and ½ cup of the granulated sugar to a boil and cook to 320° F. (hard crack stage). Immediately toss in the plum sections, stirring constantly. Add the scrapings from the vanilla bean and the brandy and cook for 1 minute, stirring to dissolve clumps of sugar. Pour the contents of the pan through a strainer into a bowl, reserving the liquid, and spread the fruit out onto a baking sheet to cool.

2. Mix together the bread crumbs, the remaining ¼ cup of granulated sugar, the nutmeg, and cinnamon.

3. Line a baking sheet with parchment paper. Carefully peel off 1 sheet of phyllo, keeping the rest moist under a damp towel, and lay on a flat surface. Using a clean spray bottle, quickly spray water into the air directly above the phyllo, letting the mist float gently down. Dip a pastry brush into the melted butter and lightly splatter the phyllo. Sprinkle heavily with the crumb mixture and top with a second sheet of phyllo. Repeat and top with a third sheet.

4. Using a ruler and a sharp knife, cut the stacked sheets into four 5½-inch squares. In the center of each square circle 3 slices of plums tightly together, skin sides out. Bring the 4 corners up and lightly press together, making an indentation to form a neck (see Note). Press tightly enough for the phyllo to stick together but not so tightly that the center layers of dough will not cook. Place the bundles on the baking sheet. Repeat 3 more times. You should have 16 bundles in all, with enough plum slices left to make the sauce.

5. Preheat the oven to 350° F.

6. When all the bundles are ready, put the baking sheet into the oven for 25 to 30 minutes, until the bundles are golden brown all over. Once baked, the bundles can be left at room temperature for 4 to 6 hours before serving.

7. To make the plum sauce, in a food processer or blender puree the remaining plum slices with just enough of the reserved liquid to make a medium-thick sauce. Add the almond extract.

8. To serve, coat each dessert plate with yogurt and swirl in 2 tablespoons of plum sauce. Top with 2 plum bundles and sprinkle with a dusting of confectioners' sugar.

Serves 8

Note: If you find the bundles are too thick at the neck, carefully snip away a little phyllo before baking or cut the top square in the stack a little smaller than the first two.

Chilled Summer Berries in Port Wine Syrup

The base of this dessert is a peppery syrup that is also part of the Strawberry Fool (page 270). Because of the dark, blue-red color of the syrup, berries are a better choice than lighter-colored summer fruits. Serve this in glass bowls with a crisp cookie or spoon it over ice cream or zabaglione.

PORT WINE SYRUP
2 cups port wine (not tawny port)
One 3-inch cinnamon stick
2 whole cloves
1 vanilla bean, split and scraped
⅛ teaspoon freshly grated nutmeg
12 whole peppercorns, cracked
1 teaspoon grated lemon zest
2 tablespoons lemon juice
⅓ cup sugar
1 cup boysenberries
1 cup raspberries
2 cups blueberries
2 cups strawberries

1. In a shallow pan combine the port with the rest of the ingredients, except the berries. Bring to a boil over high heat and reduce to 1 cup, which will take about 20 minutes. Remove from the heat and let stand for 15 minutes. Strain into a medium bowl.

2. Add half of the boysenberries and raspberries, and crush the fruit with the back of a large spoon. Stir in the remaining berries, except the strawberries. Cover and chill for 2 to 3 hours or overnight.

3. Just before serving, slice the strawberries and stir them into the fruit mixture. Spoon into glass bowls or goblets.

Serves 6

Strawberry Fool

"Fool" used to be a term of endearment. Now we reserve that old-fashioned fondness for a simple fruit and cream dessert of the same name.

2 pints strawberries or other berries
2 cups Port Wine Syrup (page 269)
2 cups heavy cream
1 cup Crème Fraîche (page 248) or sour cream

1. Reserve several perfect strawberries for garnish. Hull the rest, slice the through the stem end, and place in a nonreactive bowl. Pour the warm syrup through a strainer over the berries, crushing the fruit gently with a fork. Set aside for 30 minutes at room temperature or 1 hour in the refrigerator.

2. When ready to serve, beat the heavy cream to soft peaks and mix in the Crème Fraîche or sour cream. Remove the berries from the liquid with a slotted spoon and carefully fold them into the cream.

3. Spoon a small puddle of the syrup onto individual dessert plates or into wine goblets and top with cream and berries. Drizzle a little syrup over the cream and garnish with the reserved strawberries.

Serves 8

Plum-Rhubarb Crisp

Tart, late spring rhubarb and sweet early summer red plums come together for a simple, homey dessert. Use the Elephant Heart variety if available.

STREUSEL
1 cup sugar
¾ cup all-purpose flour
1 teaspoon ground cinnamon
1 teaspoon freshly grated nutmeg
¼ teaspoon ground cardamom
8 tablespoons (1 stick) unsalted butter, cut into 8 pieces

6 red plums, unpeeled, pitted, and cut into sixths (about 1½ pounds)
½ cup port wine (not tawny port)
1 tablespoon cornstarch dissolved in 2 tablespoons port
½ pound rhubarb, cut into ½-inch pieces
Whipped cream or ice cream

1. To make the streusel, combine all the ingredients in a food processor fitted with the metal blade and process just until the mixture holds together when pressed between the fingers. It will still appear dry and granular. Set aside or refrigerate until ready to use.

2. In a medium skillet over high heat lightly brown the plums, stirring constantly for 2 minutes. Add the port and bring to a boil. Add the dissolved cornstarch and stir to coat the plums. Quickly stir in the rhubarb and combine. Remove from the heat and mound in a 9- or 8-inch-square pan or baking dish. Cool to room temperature.

3. Preheat the oven to 425° F.

4. Place the baking dish on a cookie sheet. Distribute the streusel evenly over the top of the fruit, clumping some together. Be sure to cover the fruit completely. Bake for 25 minutes, until the streusel is lightly browned. Let stand for 10 minutes. Serve with lightly whipped cream or vanilla ice cream.

Serves 6

Strawberries in Beaujolais Sauce

An intensely red dessert sauce that is as simple in its ingredients as in its method.

6 tablespoons sugar
2 tablespoons water
One 3-inch cinnamon stick
1 vanilla bean, split and scraped
10 whole black peppercorns
2 whole cloves
1 bottle (750 ml) Beaujolais or similar red wine
6 cups strawberries
Vanilla ice cream or Strawberry Ice Cream (recipe follows)

1. In a heavy-bottomed 1½-quart saucepan stir together the sugar, water, cinnamon stick, vanilla bean, peppercorns, and cloves. Bring to a boil, without stirring again, and cook until the mixture is a dark caramel color. Remove from the heat and immediately pour in the wine. Be careful to avoid spattering. Stir well to remelt the caramel. Cook over high heat until the liquid is reduced by about half, about 20 minutes. Strain it into a bowl. Discard the spices left in the strainer.

2. Hull the strawberries and slice them lengthwise ¼ inch thick. Pour the wine sauce into a 10-inch sauté pan, bring to a boil, add the strawberries, and cook over high heat for 5 minutes, until the strawberries are soft and dark red. With a slotted spoon remove to rimmed dessert plates. Reduce the sauce over high heat to thicken it. Pour the sauce over the berries. Serve warm or at room temperature, topped with a scoop of ice cream.

Serves 6

Strawberry Ice Cream

This recipe is for everyone who is nervous about making a custard-based ice cream for fear it will curdle. There are no eggs in this recipe, and there is less cream than usual. The richness comes from cooking down the milk and cream.

1½ cups milk
½ cup heavy cream
1½ tablespoons plus about 1 cup sugar
2½ tablespoons light corn syrup
4 cups very ripe strawberries, stemmed
3 tablespoons lemon juice

1. In a heavy 2-quart stainless steel saucepan over medium-high heat boil the milk, cream, 1½ tablespoons of the sugar, and 1½ teaspoons of the corn syrup for 20 to 25 minutes, stirring occasionally, until the mixture coats a spoon. Do not allow the mixture to burn or color. Remove from the heat and cool completely.

2. Meanwhile, puree the strawberries in a blender or food processor. Stir in the lemon juice and the remaining 2 tablespoons of corn syrup. Gradually mix in the remaining sugar, adding up to 1 cup, depending on the flavor of the strawberries.

3. Stir the strawberry mixture into the cream mixture and pour into the container of an ice-cream maker. Freeze according to manufacturer's instructions. Transfer to a freezer container, cover, and leave in the freezer for up to 4 hours.

Makes about 1½ quarts

Lemon Ice Cream

Nancy's tastes have changed about ice creams since her first book; she now prefers a less rich, colder version. The thinner the texture, the colder the ice cream will become. The color of this ice cream is almost white, but the flavor is boldly lemon. It's wonderful with Plum Bundles (page 266).

3 large lemons
2 cups heavy cream
2 cups milk
4 egg yolks
¾ cup sugar
½ cup lemon juice

1. With a zester or very sharp knife remove just the outer skin of the lemons in long shreds, being careful not to include the white pith.

2. In a medium saucepan bring the cream to just below a boil, add the lemon zest, and remove from the heat. Cover and allow to steep for 1 hour or more. Strain into another pan, discard the zest, and reheat the cream with the milk.

3. In a small bowl whisk together the egg yolks and sugar. Pour a little of the hot cream into the yolks, then pour all of the yolk mixture into the cream. Return to medium heat. Cook, stirring constantly, until the custard is thick enough to coat the back of a wooden spoon, about 2 to 3 minutes. Remove from the heat. Stir in the lemon juice and cool to room temperature. Cover and refrigerate until ready to freeze.

4. Pour into the container of an ice-cream maker. Freeze according to manufacturer's directions. Transfer to a freezer container, cover, and leave in the freezer until ready to serve.

Makes 1 quart

Tangerine Ice Cream

This pale orange ice cream is close to a sherbet in consistency. By using corn syrup, you can incorporate a large amount of fresh tangerine juice without having the texture become icy. The zest is very important here for color, but remember that too much can taste bitter. This ice cream takes longer than others to freeze smoothly, and it never becomes completely hard. Tangerines are best squeezed by hand; since the peel is loose, it is difficult to hold the fruit over a juicer.

7½ pounds medium tangerines, preferably Dancy or Satsuma
1 cup milk
1 cup heavy cream
1 vanilla bean, split and scraped
¼ cup grated tangerine zest
¼ cup sugar
4 egg yolks
⅓ cup light corn syrup

1. Juice the tangerines. You should have 3 cups.

2. Bring the milk, cream, vanilla bean, and zest to just below a boil. Turn off the heat, cover, and allow to steep for 1 hour. Strain.

3. Whisk the sugar and egg yolks together. Reheat the cream and whisk a small amount into the yolks. Pour the mixture back into the cream and place over medium heat. Cook, stirring constantly, until the mixture coats the back of a wooden spoon, 2 to 3 minutes. Remove from the heat and stir in the juice and ¼ cup of the corn syrup. Taste. If not sweet enough, add another tablespoon of corn syrup. Cover and chill several hours or overnight.

4. Pour into the container of an ice-cream maker and freeze according to manufacturer's instructions. Transfer to a freezer container, cover, and leave in the freezer until ready to serve.

Makes 1½ quarts

Espresso Ice Cream

For real coffee lovers. We use whole beans and freshly brewed coffee to achieve a distinctively strong infusion. Serve with a chocolate cake or Panforte (page 287). Ice cream made from espresso is often grainy, but the corn syrup keeps this one smooth.

2 cups heavy cream
2 cups whole milk
1 cup decaffeinated espresso beans, crushed with a rolling pin
1 vanilla bean, split and scraped
8 egg yolks
½ cup sugar
1 cup freshly brewed espresso
½ cup light corn syrup

1. In a medium saucepan bring the cream, milk, crushed beans, and vanilla bean to just below a boil. Turn off the heat, cover, and steep for 30 minutes. Strain.

2. In a medium bowl whisk the egg yolks and sugar together. Pour ½ cup of warm cream into the yolks while whisking, then pour back into the saucepan. Cook over medium heat, stirring constantly, until the mixture is thick enough to coat the back of a wooden spoon, about 2 to 3 minutes. Remove from the heat and whisk in the espresso and corn syrup. Cool to room temperature, cover, and refrigerate until well chilled, for several hours or overnight.

3. Pour into the container of an ice-cream maker and freeze according to manufacturer's directions. Transfer to a freezer container, cover, and keep frozen until ready to serve.

Makes 1½ quarts

Blood Orange Sherbet Dessert

There's a short time in January when the pomegranate and blood orange seasons overlap. That's the time to make this spectacular dessert.

BLOOD ORANGE SHERBET
12 large blood oranges
2 tablespoons light corn syrup
½ cup sugar
1 teaspoon freshly ground black pepper
¼ cup lemon juice

6 blood oranges
1 cup water
1 cup sugar
1 tablespoon corn syrup
⅓ cup fresh pomegranate seeds
6 dried Black Mission figs, cut lengthwise into eighths

1. To make the sherbet, squeeze the 12 oranges; you should have 2 cups of juice. Strain and remove pits. Pour the juice into a bowl and add the corn syrup, sugar, pepper, and lemon juice. Pour into an ice-cream maker and freeze according to manufacturer's directions. Transfer to a container, cover, and freeze until ready to serve.

2. Remove the zest of 6 oranges in long shreds and reserve. In a small saucepan bring the water, sugar, and corn syrup to a boil and add the zest. Turn down the heat and simmer for 20 to 25 minutes, until the zest is translucent. Set aside.

3. Cut away the white pith of the oranges and discard. Separate the oranges into sections by cutting on both sides of the membranes that divide the sections. Squeeze any juice from the membrane and combine with the orange slices.

4. To serve, divide the sections and juice among 6 soup plates. Mound the sherbet in the center of each plate, strew with candied zest, and add the pomegranate seeds and figs.

Makes about 3 cups

Ricotta Cheesecake

This recipe is extremely light and smooth with none of the dryness usually associated with ricotta cheese. To avoid the soggy crust that so often lines a cheesecake pan, we bake a crust separately, like a huge cookie, and cut it into wedges. Wisps of pine nut brittle decorate the top of the cake. If you're short on time, the cheesecake can stand alone.

1 teaspoon finely chopped lemon zest
1½ tablespoons lemon juice
1 cup pure ricotta, preferably whole milk (8 ounces) (see Note)
1 cup sour cream
4 tablespoons (½ stick) unsalted butter, softened
½ pound cream cheese, at room temperature
¼ cup flour
2 large eggs
1 egg yolk
1 cup sugar
1½ teaspoons pure vanilla extract
⅔ cup dried fruit, such as blueberries, sour cherries, cranberries, golden raisins, chopped prunes, or a combination of fruits
½ cup pine nuts, coarsely chopped
Crust for Ricotta Cheesecake (recipe follows)
Pine Nut Brittle for Ricotta Cheesecake (recipe follows)

1. Preheat the oven to 275° F. Butter and flour a 9- or 9½-inch springform pan.

2. In the bowl of an electric mixer fitted with the whisk attachment, beat together the zest, lemon juice, ricotta, and sour cream. Set aside. In another bowl of the mixer, with the paddle attachment beat the butter until fluffy, scraping the sides of the bowl occasionally. Add the cream cheese and beat on high speed until smooth. Add the flour and continue beating for 2 minutes. Remove the bowl from the mixer and fold in the ricotta mixture.

3. Wash the first bowl and with the whisk attachment beat the eggs, egg yolk, sugar, and vanilla on high speed for 3 minutes, until whitened. Remove from the mixer. Fold the dried fruit into the ricotta mixture, then combine with the egg mixture until completely incorporated. Pour into the prepared pan and sprinkle with pine nuts.

4. Bake for 2 hours, until the pine nuts and top of the cake are lightly browned, without opening the oven door during the first hour of baking. Turn off the oven and leave the cheesecake in the oven for an additional hour. The cheesecake should be in the oven a total of 3 hours. Remove from the oven and serve within 30 minutes. (The cheesecake is at its best served warm.) To serve, cut the cheesecake into wedges and slide a piece onto a wedge of crust. Decorate the top with brittle.

Serves 10

Note: The purest, freshest ricotta is sold in kosher markets. Read the ingredients on the label to be sure there are no stabilizers, gelatin, or preservatives. This will insure freshness and a softer, creamier texture.

Crust for Ricotta Cheesecake

This crust underlies the soft, warm cheesecake slice without becoming soggy. It can be baked a day ahead but must be wrapped tightly in plastic wrap to stay crisp.

1 cup whole unblanched almonds
3 tablespoons sugar
4 tablespoons (½ stick) unsalted butter, cold
5 tablespoons all-purpose flour

1. Preheat the oven to 350° F. Line a baking sheet with parchment paper.
2. In a food processor fitted with the metal blade finely grind the almonds with the sugar. Add the butter and process until combined. Add the flour and process just until incorporated. Form into a ball, wrap in plastic, and chill until firm.
3. Remove from the refrigerator and pound with a rolling pin to flatten into a 10-inch circle, ¼ inch thick. If the dough cracks it is probably too cold—press the palms of your hands on the dough to warm it up. If the dough tears when rolled out, pat it back together with your hands. Carefully transfer the dough to the baking sheet. Bake for 10 minutes, until golden brown.
4. Remove from the oven and cool for 2 minutes. Cut the circle into 10 equal wedges. Carefully transfer each wedge to a cooling rack. If the crust is too cool it will stick to the baking sheet and crumble when removed. If that happens, return the pan to the warm oven, reheat slightly, and remove the remaining pieces.

Pine Nut Brittle
for Ricotta Cheesecake

Pulled strands of this amber-colored brittle must be prepared just a few hours before serving. Don't try it in humid weather.

2 cups water
Zest of 3 lemons, in long shreds
1 tablespoon vegetable oil
½ cup sugar
¼ cup pine nuts

1. Bring the water to a boil and drop in the zest. Boil for 1 minute, drain, and rinse under cold water. Spread out on paper towels to dry. Lightly oil the back of a cookie sheet and pat dry. Set aside.

2. In a heavy small saucepan melt the sugar over medium heat. Watching carefully as it begins to color, swirl the pan to distribute evenly. When the sugar completely liquefies and is golden, stir in the pine nuts. If the sugar starts to darken too much, remove from the heat. Continue stirring until the pine nuts are evenly light brown. Add the zest and cook for 1 minute. Immediately pour out onto the oiled baking sheet and allow to cool *slightly*.

3. When just cool enough to handle (the mixture will still be fairly hot), begin to pick up the corners with a butter knife and stretch the brittle into paper-thin sheets with wispy edges. Place each piece on a baking sheet or large plate.

Variation: Chopped walnuts, pumpkins seeds, or sliced blanched almonds can be substituted for the pine nuts.

Espresso Milk Shake

About three years ago Nancy and both of the kids came down with the chicken pox at the same time. Nancy was the most miserable because she had chicken pox even down her throat. So that Nancy could continue to consume her daily three cappuccinos, Mark invented this Expresso Milk Shake for her. Although she went back to drinking hot cappuccino when she recovered, Nancy still likes the occasional milk shake for dessert.

½ cup full-strength espresso, chilled
2 tablespoons light corn syrup
½ cup heavy cream, chilled
1 pint vanilla ice cream, slightly softened

In a blender on low speed blend together the espresso, corn syrup, and heavy cream. Spoon half of the ice cream into the blender and beat on high speed until incorporated. Add the remaining ice cream and continue running the machine until the mixture is completely emulsified and very smooth. Pour into 2 tall glasses and serve.

Serves 2

Chocolate Soufflé Cake

This is a majestic cake, and depending on what liquid you choose—coffee, Grand Marnier, bourbon whiskey, or orange juice—can taste very adult or just rich and chocolatey for younger eaters.

12 tablespoons (1½ sticks) unsalted butter, cold
1½ cups sugar
4 eggs, separated, at room temperature
1 tablespoon pure vanilla extract
11 ounces imported bittersweet chocolate, such as Tobler or
    Lindt, melted
⅓ cup orange juice, coffee, Grand Marnier, bourbon whiskey,
    or water
1¼ cups cake flour
1 teaspoon baking soda dissolved in 1 tablespoon boiling water

GARNISH
Confectioners' sugar, sifted
Crème Fraîche (page 248) or whipped cream (optional)

1. Preheat the oven to 350° F. Grease the inside of an 8-inch springform pan or cake ring. If using a cake ring, cover an unwarped cookie sheet with foil.

2. In an electric mixer on low speed, with the paddle attachment cream the butter and ¾ cup of the sugar. With the mixer on low speed, add the egg yolks and vanilla, beating until combined. Stir in the chocolate, liquid, and half of the flour. When these are incorporated, add the remaining flour and dissolved baking soda.

3. In a separate mixing bowl beat the egg whites on low speed until white and foamy. Turn up to high speed and gradually add the remaining ½ cup of sugar, beating until the mixture is shiny and thick, like marshmallow cream. Stir two-thirds of the whites into the chocolate batter, then fold in the remaining whites. The batter should be uniformly mixed and very smooth.

4. Pour the batter into the springform pan or place the cake ring on the cookie sheet and pour in the batter. Place in the upper third of the oven and bake for 50 to 55 minutes, without opening the oven door for the first 20 minutes. The cake may rise slightly above the edge of the ring.

5. Remove from the oven and run a paring knife along the inside edge of the ring. Immediately invert onto a serving plate. Allow the cake to cool to room temperature. Remove the ring or the sides and bottom of the springform pan.

6. When ready to serve, dust heavily with confectioners' sugar. Serve each slice with Crème Fraîche or unsweetened whipped cream, if desired. Best served the same day.

Serves **6** *to* **8**

Panforte

This Italian after-dinner sweet is a nutty, chewy fruitcake. Any combination of dried fruits will work as long as the total weight of the fruit is one and one-quarter pounds. At Campanile we serve a wedge of this confection with Espresso Ice Cream (page 277) and Almond Biscotti (page 297).

6 ounces whole unblanched almonds
6 ounces whole unblanched hazelnuts
2 tablespoons ground cinnamon
½ teaspoon ground ginger
¼ teaspoon ground cloves
1 cup plus 2 tablespoons all-purpose flour
1½ teaspoons unsweetened cocoa powder
1 cup sugar
⅔ cup honey
1¼ pounds dried organic fruits, any combination of apricots,
    figs, raisins, cranberries, cherries, prunes, and pineapple
    (see Note)

GARNISH
Confectioners' sugar

1. Preheat the oven to 350° F.

2. Keeping them separate on a cookie sheet, toast the almonds and hazelnuts for 10 minutes, until lightly browned. Remove from the oven and reduce the oven temperature to 300° F. Place the hazelnuts in a dry towel and rub to remove the skins. Leave skins on the almonds.

3. In a large bowl toss the nuts with the cinnamon, ginger, cloves, flour, and cocoa powder. Cut the fruits into ½-inch pieces and add, stirring to combine.

4. In a small saucepan over high heat bring the sugar and honey to a full boil and cook to 225° F. (soft ball stage). Immediately pour into the fruit mixture and stir. The dough will be very stiff.

5. Generously butter and dust with flour or cocoa powder a 9-inch springform pan or 9 × 1-inch flan ring placed on a parchment-lined baking sheet. With buttered or wet hands, press the fruit mixture evenly into the pan. Bake for 1 hour, until the edges look set and the top is slightly puffed. Remove from the oven and cool completely in the pan.

6. Run a knife around the edges of the pan and remove the sides. Store at room temperature. Wrapped tightly in plastic wrap, panforte will keep for several weeks. Before serving, dust with confectioners' sugar and slice into thin wedges.

Serves 16

Note: If the fruit is dry and hard, pour on boiling water to cover and let soften. Drain before using.

Bittersweet Chocolate Mousse

Especially in our house, saying that chocolate mousse will keep for several days in the refrigerator is like saying, "Here is a present for you but don't open it." Be sure to use a bittersweet chocolate of the very best quality.

12 eggs, separated
¼ cup honey
¼ cup dark rum
1 pound imported bittersweet chocolate, such as Tobler Extra
      Bittersweet, Lindt, or Callebaut, melted
½ cup heavy cream
½ cup sugar

GARNISH
Whipped cream
Cocoa powder

1. In a large metal bowl placed over a shallow pot of simmering water, whisk the egg yolks and honey until the mixture thickens and forms a ribbon when the whisk is lifted, 7 to 8 minutes. Make sure the water is not so hot that it cooks the eggs. Remove from the heat and cool. It should feel the same temperature as your finger. Stir in the rum and half of the chocolate.

2. In a medium bowl whisk the heavy cream or pour it into the bowl of an electric mixer and beat until softly whipped. Add to the chocolate mixture.

3. In a clean bowl beat the egg whites until foamy. Gradually add the sugar and beat until the mixture is stiff, shiny, and thick, like marshmallow cream. Add half of the whites to the chocolate mixture and whisk until no streaks remain. Add the remaining egg whites, beating until completely incorporated. Stir in the remaining melted chocolate.

4. Spoon into a large bowl, swirl the top, cover with plastic wrap, and refrigerate for several hours or overnight before serving.

5. To serve, spoon out individual portions with a large oval spoon or ice cream scoop. Serve with whipped cream and a dusting of cocoa powder.

Serves 12

Caramel Rice Flan

This elegant dish has all the aromas and flavors of homey rice pudding. Arborio rice stays much creamier and softer than regular rice because it tends to absorb more liquid in the initial cooking. Nancy likes to garnish the flan with Brandy Snaps (page 303).

1 cup sugar
¼ cup water
¼ cup Arborio rice
1½ cups milk
1 vanilla bean, split and scraped
One 3-inch cinnamon stick
¼ teaspoon freshly grated nutmeg
⅛ teaspoon ground cardamom

CUSTARD
2 cups milk
2 eggs
4 egg yolks
⅓ cup sugar
1 vanilla bean, split and scraped

1. In a heavy small saucepan stir together the sugar and water and bring to a boil. Cook over high heat for 5 to 8 minutes, until the mixture turns mahogany brown. Immediately pour into six ½-cup ramekins. Set aside to harden.

2. Preheat the oven to 350° F.

3. In a medium saucepan bring the rice and milk to a boil. Add the vanilla bean, cinnamon, nutmeg, and cardamom. Cook until the rice is barely tender, about 15 minutes, stirring occasionally. Drain and rinse the rice under hot water. Remove and discard the cinnamon stick. Set aside.

4. To make the custard, in a medium saucepan bring the milk and vanilla bean to a boil. In a medium bowl whisk together the eggs, yolks, and sugar. Slowly pour the hot milk into the egg mixture, whisking constantly. Strain the mixture back into the pan and remove from the heat.

5. Divide the rice among the ramekins, pressing down to cover the caramel. Pour in the custard. Place the ramekins in a large roasting pan and fill with water to come three-quarters of the way up the sides. Cover tightly with foil and punch several steam holes in it. Place the pan in the center of the oven and bake for 25 to 30 minutes, or until the custard is set around the edges but the center still jiggles. Remove from the water bath, and refrigerate until set and cold.

6. To serve, dip each ramekin into hot water, run a knife around the edge, and turn it out onto a dessert plate.

Serves 6

Variation: To make the flan in a 1½-quart soufflé dish, use 4 eggs and 2 yolks for the custard. The rest of the ingredients remain the same. Increase the cooking time to 35 minutes. Chill well before inverting.

Kahlúa Flan

Nothing is quite so satisfying at the end of a meal as sweetened coffee and cream. Here those tastes are combined in a tender melt-in-your-mouth flan.

¾ cup sugar
2 tablespoons water

FLAN
1¾ cups milk
¼ cup half-and-half
1 tablespoon instant espresso powder
3 eggs
4 egg yolks
¼ cup sugar
⅓ cup Kahlúa or other coffee-flavored liqueur

1. In a small heavy saucepan over high heat stir together the sugar and water. Bring to a boil and cook, without stirring, until the mixture turns mahogany brown, about 5 to 8 minutes. Immediately pour into a 1½-quart soufflé dish, turning to coat halfway up the sides. Set aside to harden.

2. Preheat the oven to 325° F.

3. In a medium saucepan over medium heat warm the milk and half-and-half. Add the espresso powder and stir until dissolved.

4. In a medium bowl gently whisk the eggs, egg yolks, and sugar together while slowly adding the warm milk mixture. Stir in the Kahlúa. Pour through a strainer into the caramel-lined dish.

5. Place the dish in a shallow roasting pan and fill with warm water to come halfway up the sides. Cover the pan tightly with foil and with the tip of a knife punch about 6 holes for steam vents. Place the pan on the center rack of the oven and bake for 45 to 55 minutes, until a knife inserted in the center comes out clean but the center still jiggles slightly. Remove from the water bath and cool to room temperature. Chill before serving.

6. To serve use the tip of a knife to loosen the sides of the flan. Place a rimmed plate on top of the dish and invert.

Serves 6

Yam and Persimmon Flan

Yams and persimmons seem to have a natural affinity for one another. They are abundantly available at the same time of year and their orange colors complement one another beautifully. This dish is really a pudding, but its custardlike texture allows it to be served like a flan. It is also delicious cold. It becomes a bit denser, but this way it can be made a day ahead and refrigerated overnight.

PRALINE

½ cup sugar
¼ cup water
½ cup pecan pieces

PUDDING

6 eggs
½ cup sugar
¼ cup honey
1 pound very soft persimmons, pulp scooped from skin (about
    3 medium Hachiya or 4 small Fuyu persimmons)
2 pounds yams, baked, peeled, and mashed
1½ cups all-purpose flour
½ teaspoon coarse salt
2 teaspoons ground cinnamon
1 teaspoon ground ginger
½ teaspoon ground cloves
1 teaspoon baking soda
1 teaspoon baking powder
6 tablespoons (¾ stick) unsalted butter, melted
2 cups light cream or half-and-half

GARNISH

1 cup heavy cream, lightly whipped

1. Lightly oil the back of a cookie sheet. In a heavy-bottomed small saucepan stir together the sugar and water and cook, without stirring, over medium heat until the mixture turns medium brown. Quickly add the pecans and cook, stirring to coat the nuts evenly, for 1 to 2 minutes. Pour out onto the cookie sheet and spread thinly, distributing evenly. Set aside to harden and cool completely.

2. With a spatula, transfer the praline to a cutting board and coarsely chop. (The praline can be prepared up to 1 week in advance and stored, tightly covered.) Sprinkle this mixture evenly over the bottom of a 9-inch springform pan.

3. Preheat the oven to 350° F.

4. To make the pudding, in the bowl of a mixer on high beat together the eggs, sugar, and honey until light and foamy. Turn the mixer to low and add the persimmon pulp, yams, melted butter, and half-and-half. In a separate bowl stir together the flour, salt, cinnamon, ginger, cloves, baking soda, and baking powder. With the mixer on low add the dry ingredients to the egg mixture in batches. When the ingredients are well incorporated, pour the batter into the praline-lined pan. The batter will be thin and will come close to the top of the pan. Place the pan on a cookie sheet and bake in the center of the oven for 1 hour 15 minutes, until the edges look browned and crisp and a knife inserted in the center comes out clean. The pudding will have risen slightly above the rim of the pan.

5. Remove from the oven and allow to cool 1 hour, to room temperature. The pudding will fall somewhat. Run a knife around the springform pan to loosen the sides.

6. To serve, place on a rimmed plate and remove the sides of the pan. Cut the pudding into wedges and garnish with whipped cream.

Serves 8 to 10

Almond Biscotti

In Italy these dry, nonsweet cookies are traditionally served with cappuccino or a sweet dessert wine. Some people dunk them in their coffee. We prefer this version, which has a slightly softer texture than usual, as well as the crunch of pumpkin seeds and anise seeds.

4 tablespoons (½ stick) unsalted butter
1 vanilla bean, split and scraped
1 egg yolk
½ cup sugar
¼ teaspoon grated lemon zest
2 teaspoons pure almond extract
1½ cups all-purpose flour
½ teaspoon baking powder
3 egg whites
⅔ cup whole toasted almonds
⅓ cup toasted pumpkin seeds
1 tablespoon anise seed

1. Preheat the oven to 325° F. Line a baking sheet with parchment paper.
2. In a small pan melt the butter with the seeds and pod of the vanilla bean. Set aside and remove and discard the pod.

3. In an electric mixer with the paddle attachment combine the egg yolk with ¼ cup of the sugar. Stir in the melted butter, zest, and almond extract. Add the flour and baking powder and mix until the batter appears crumbly but uniformly mixed. In a separate bowl beat 2 of the egg whites with the remaining sugar. Fold in the flour mixture, and with the machine on low pour in the almonds and pumpkin seeds. Gather the dough into a ball and shape into a log about 15 inches long. Place on the baking sheet. Brush with the remaining egg white and sprinkle the top with anise seed.

4. Bake for 30 minutes and remove from the oven. The log will still feel soft to the touch. Cool completely. Turn the oven down to 250° F. With a serrated knife, slice the log on the diagonal every ⅓ inch. Place the slices on the baking sheet and bake for 1 hour, until pale golden. Cool and store in an airtight tin. Biscotti will keep for 4 or 5 days, but for best flavor rebake again before serving.

Makes 16 to 18 biscotti

Greek Walnut Cookies

Kerry Caloyannidis, our assistant pastry chef when Campanile opened, was inspired by her Greek father to develop this recipe. Ground walnuts give this cookie the texture of nutty shortbread. After baking, a honey-sweetened syrup is poured over the cookies for additional flavor and a glossy look like that of baklava.

4 tablespoons Clarified Butter (page 168)
⅓ cup plus 1 tablespoon walnut oil
2 tablespoons white wine
2 tablespoons rum
2 teaspoons pure vanilla extract
2 cups plus 2 tablespoons cake flour
½ teaspoon baking powder
1¼ cups finely ground walnuts
⅓ cup plus 1 tablespoon sugar
½ teaspoon ground cinnamon

SYRUP
1 cup sugar
¾ cup water
½ teaspoon grated lemon zest
5 whole cloves
One 3-inch cinnamon stick
1 tablespoon rum
½ cup honey

GARNISH
¼ cup finely chopped walnuts

1. Preheat the oven to 350° F. Line baking sheets with parchment paper.
2. In a large bowl stir together the butter, walnut oil, wine, rum, and vanilla. Add the flour, baking powder, ground walnuts, sugar, and cinnamon and combine until the mixture resembles wet sand. With your hands, form the dough into ovals ½ × 1 × ½ inch.

3. Place on baking sheets in the center of the oven and bake for 30 minutes, until light brown on the bottom. Cookies will expand somewhat.

4. Meanwhile, in a medium saucepan stir together all the ingredients for the syrup and bring to a boil. Remove from the heat and strain. Discard the cloves and cinnamon stick.

5. Remove the hot cookies from the baking sheet to a rack set over a cookie sheet. Carefully pour the hot syrup over the tops of the cookies, using all the syrup. Sprinkle with finely chopped walnuts. Cool completely. Cookies will keep, in a single layer, tightly covered for up to 5 days.

Makes about 50 cookies

ANZAC Cookies

In Australia this light and crunchy cookie is equal in popularity to our own chocolate chip cookie. Traditionally, it was a homemade cookie that was baked for soldiers (ANZAC stands for Australian and New Zealand Army Corps) as well as for children coming home from school. This recipe was given to us by our former assistant pastry chef, Australian Kerry Caloyannidis.

6 tablespoons (¾ stick) unsalted butter
½ cup rolled oats
½ cup unsweetened coconut (see Note)
6 tablespoons all-purpose flour
5 tablespoons sugar
½ teaspoon baking soda dissolved in 1 tablespoon boiling
    water
½ teaspoon grated lemon zest

1. Preheat the oven to 350° F.

2. In a medium saucepan over medium heat melt 2 tablespoons of the butter and stir in the oats. Cook, stirring often, until the oats are lightly browned. Cut the remaining butter into small pieces and add to the pan. Remove from the heat and stir until the butter is melted.

3. Spread out the coconut on a baking sheet and bake for 5 to 7 minutes, until lightly toasted.

4. Add the flour, sugar, dissolved baking soda, zest, and coconut to the oats and butter. Stir together and let cool to room temperature.

5. Line a baking sheet with parchment paper. Shape the dough into 1-inch balls (you should have about 20) and place on the baking sheet. Press down on each ball to flatten. Bake for 15 minutes, until lightly golden. Cool for 5 minutes before removing from the pan. Store in an airtight tin rather than a cookie jar.

Makes about twenty 2½-inch cookies

Note: Unsweetened coconut is available in health-food stores.

Creamy Potato Brownies

To create an entirely new brownie was a challenge. Potatoes were the answer. With their high starch and moisture content, potatoes give brownies a smooth texture without interfering with the flavor of the chocolate. Right out of the refrigerator, they are cool and creamy. Served at room temperature with a drizzle of chocolate sauce and a scoop of ice cream, they are moist and fudgy. This is not a brownie that is so dense and rich you can take only one bite.

1¼ pounds imported bittersweet chocolate, such as Tobler's Tradition
8 tablespoons (1 stick) unsalted butter
3 very small red potatoes (¼ pound)
4 large eggs
¾ cup sugar
1 tablespoon pure vanilla extract
6 tablespoons cake flour
1½ cups coarsely chopped walnuts

1. Preheat the oven to 375° F. Butter an 8-inch-square baking pan and sprinkle with cocoa powder.

2. In the top of a double boiler melt 1 pound of the chocolate and the butter together over simmering water. Set aside.

3. Peel the potatoes and cut each in half. Boil in water to cover until tender, about 15 minutes. Drain.

4. In a food processor fitted with the metal blade, process the eggs, sugar, and vanilla until creamy and light. Add the warm potatoes and process until no chunks remain. Pulse in the melted chocolate until incorporated. Sprinkle the flour over the batter and pulse to combine. Coarsely chop the remaining ¼ pound of chocolate. Add the chocolate and walnuts to the dough and pulse to combine.

5. Pour the batter into the baking pan, smooth the top, and bake in the center of the oven for 30 to 35 minutes, until the top feels firm to the touch. Remove from the oven and cool to room temperature. Invert onto a plate, reverse onto heavy foil, wrap securely, and refrigerate overnight. Cut into 2-inch squares.

Makes 16 brownies

Brandy Snaps

These lacy cookies are a little tricky but so delicate and beautiful that the extra care is justified. Don't even try to make them on a humid day; they will not become crisp. Begin by baking one cookie at a time. Once you're familiar with the timing, drop a few onto the baking sheet. Scrunch the warm cookies into free-form shapes and serve them with ice cream and flan.

8 tablespoons (1 stick) unsalted butter
½ cup light corn syrup
½ cup (firmly packed) dark brown sugar
⅔ cup all-purpose flour
1 tablespoon ground ginger

1. Preheat the oven to 350° F. Generously butter a Teflon-coated or regular baking sheet and keep it warm.

2. In a saucepan over medium heat melt together the butter, corn syrup, and brown sugar. Remove from the heat and let cool for several minutes. Stir in the flour and ginger. This dough may be made a few days in advance and refrigerated.

3. Drop the dough by level tablespoonfuls onto the baking sheet. Bake for 4 to 5 minutes, until bubbly. Remove from the oven and allow to rest for about 40 seconds on the baking sheet. Carefully lift each cookie and gently crumple to resemble a rumpled sheet. If a cookie becomes too firm to shape, return the pan to the oven to soften. Allow to cool. Best served the same day as baked.

Makes 25 to 30 cookies

MENU SUGGESTIONS

ALL-AMERICAN STEAK DINNER

Peppered Steak
French Fries
Sautéed Spinach
Espresso Milk Shake

305

FAMILIAR FOOD
FOR CRANKY KIDS

Linguine with Spring Peas and Artichoke
Mixed Green Salad
ANZAC Cookies

PICNIC IN A MEADOW
OR ON THE BEACH

Southern Fried Chicken
Sautéed Zucchini Halves
Lentil Salad with Vegetables and Goat Cheese
Creamy Potato Brownies

PICNIC FOR AN EVENING CONCERT IN THE PARK

The Perfect Egg Salad Sandwich or Lamb and Feta Sandwich
Pan-charred Broccoli in Hot Chili Oil (chilled)
Stuffed Breast of Veal with Aïoli
Greek Walnut Cookies

PATIO BARBECUE

The Best Burger or Japanese Flank Steak
Grilled Skewered Vegetables or Sautéed Zucchini Halves

HALF-AWAKE WEEKDAY BREAKFAST

Potato, Fennel, and Garlic Frittata or
Creamy Scrambled Eggs with Porcini Mushrooms or
Oatmeal with Caramelized Apples or
Blueberry Muffins with Nutmeg Topping

LATE-MORNING WEEKEND BREAKFAST

Breakfast Tarte Tatin
Poached Eggs with Chicory and Bacon
Sour Cream Corn Muffins

BREAKFAST FOR HOUSEGUESTS

Twelve-Egg Frittata
Café Bran Muffins with Gingered Pear Marmalade
Chilled Summer Berries in Port Wine Syrup

THE-IN-LAWS-ARE-COMING-FOR-DINNER DINNER

Leg of Lamb, The Best
Baba Ghanoosh
Braised Bitter Greens
Potato Shoes
Ricotta Cheesecake

LIGHT LATE DINNER FOR TWO

Seared Scallops with Tomato Vinaigrette
Glazed Shallots
Rice with Toasted Flax Seed
Grilled Asparagus

SUNDAY NIGHT
SUMMER SUPPER

Sautéed Spicy Catfish
Polenta
Mixed Green Salad
Meyer Lemon Tart

CONVERSION CHART

LIQUID MEASURES

Fluid Ounces	U.S. Measures	Imperial Measures	Milliliters
	1 tsp.	1 tsp.	5
¼	2 tsp.	1 dessert spoon	7
½	1 T.	1 T.	15
1	2 T.	2 T.	28
2	¼ cup	4 T.	56
4	½ cup or ¼ pint		110
5		¼ pint or 1 gill	140
6	¾ cup		170
8	1 cup or ½ pint		225
9			250 (¼ liter)
10	1¼ cups	½ pint	280
12	1½ cups or ¾ pint		340
15		¾ pint	420
16	2 cups or 1 pint		450
18	2¼ cups		500 (½ liter)
20	2½ cups	1 pint	560
24	3 cups or 1½ pints		675
25		1¼ pints	700
27	3½ cups		750
30	3¾ cups	1½ pints	840
32	4 cups or 2 pints or 1 quart		900
35		1¾ pints	980
36	4½ cups		1000 (1 liter)

SOLID MEASURES

U.S. and Imperial Measures		Metric Measures	
Ounces	Pounds	Grams	Kilos
1		28	
2		56	
3½		100	
4	¼	112	
5		140	
6		168	
8	½	225	
9		250	¼
12	¾	340	
16	1	450	
18		500	½
20	1¼	560	
24	1½	675	
27		750	¾
28	1¾	780	
32	2	900	
36	2¼	1000	1
40		1100	
48	3	1350	
54		1500	1½

OVEN TEMPERATURE EQUIVALENTS

Fahrenheit	Gas Mark	Celsius	Heat of Oven
225	¼	107	Very Cool
250	½	121	Very Cool
275	1	135	Cool
300	2	148	Cool
325	3	163	Moderate
350	4	177	Moderate
375	5	190	Fairly Hot
400	6	204	Fairly Hot
425	7	218	Hot
450	8	232	Very Hot
475	9	246	Very Hot

INDEX